WESKER'S

Arnold Wesker's
LOVE PLAYS

THE FOUR SEASONS
LOVE LETTERS ON BLUE PAPER
LADY OTHELLO

OBERON BOOKS
LONDON

First published in 2008 by Oberon Books Ltd
521 Caledonian Road, London N7 9RH
Tel: 020 7607 3637 / Fax: 020 7607 3629
email: info@oberonbooks.com
www.oberonbooks.com

A catalogue record for this book is available from the British Library.

Cover photograph by Nobby Clark

ISBN 978-1-84002-791-4

Printed in Great Britain by Antony Rowe Ltd, Chippenham

Contents

THE FOUR SEASONS

Characters

ADAM

BEATRICE

Ages between 35 and 45

Setting

An isolated cottage in rural England

Time

The present

The Four Seasons received its world première in Havana in 1964 and was directed by the author. Its UK première starred Alan Bates and Diane Cilento and opened at The Belgrade Theatre, Coventry, in August 1965, before transferring to London's Saville Theatre where it ran for three months.

Act One

WINTER

PART 1

Two middle-aged people enter a deserted house. Cases in their hands.

ADAM and BEATRICE.

She's unhappy, listless, almost catatonic.

He's determined though not without battle scars. The difference is between his English and her middle-European nature.

The room is long and low with oak-timbered ceiling and furnished with a mixture of antiques, which, if they have any beauty, have only the beauty that accompanies neglected and sad things; and of plain furniture perhaps handmade.

A kitchen can be seen.

He switches electric switch on, off, on.

ADAM   And God said let there be light.

> *Watches her for response. None.*

We're safe, it's all right, no one lives here.

My uncle's. Retired judge. Found nature too sad. Imagine fleeing this!

You don't think anywhere is safe do you?

Won't you even say you like it? Say 'I like it'. Just those three words. Or 'I don't like it' or 'let's leave' or give a sigh, a smile. Won't you even sit down? Only if I bring you a chair.

> *He does so. Gently seats her.*

I can see you'll do nothing unless I prepare it for you. Right! Then for the first weeks I'll prepare

everything for you – your food, your bed, warm you,
just for the first weeks.

Try, please, say 'I – (*Waits.*) like – (*Waits.*) it.'

No response.

Not even three words?

Moves to the window.

Listen to that wind. Cold? I'll put a new pane in that
window tomorrow, sometime.

Finds a piece of sacking to stuff in the gap.

Wait.

Moves to old chest from which he draws two blankets.

Warm. First thing, always, is to be warm.

One he wraps round her legs.

Invalid! You *are* an invalid aren't you? Beautiful, too.

BEATRICE closes her eyes, and sleeps.

ADAM watches for a long while.

He raises his hand, about to touch her face.

No, I won't touch you. Why are sad faces such lovely
faces? Sleep. Touch you will I not.

Such a lovely face. A face I could love. Even 'love'
again. But I won't, lovely lady. Not love again. Not
all that again. I'll give you warmth but not love.
Not all those old, familiar patterns of betrayal, those
reproaches. And you know them, don't you? I can
tell as you sleep, from the lines round your eyes,
you know them. I know what you'd say if you were
awake. You'd say: 'Are you afraid? Are you afraid
of love?' And I'd say: 'Yes, I am afraid of love.' And
you'd chide me, call me coward. 'Those who are
afraid to die, die a thousand times,' you'd say. Or
some such thing. And then I'd feel mean for holding
back, and I'd give. Give and give and give, because
every part of me aches to give. No! Not again. Not
all that again.

BEATRICE wakes with a start.

Bad dreams? They'll pass. I'll get some wood for a fire. Not even three words? Just three?

Silence. He leaves to gather fuel.

She stares after him for a long time then back to look around the room. Its sadness, desolation, cold reach her. She is crying.

Her blanket falls to the floor, she slides from the chair to her knees, hugs the blanket to her.

ADAM returns, stands by the door, makes no move towards her. Then, sternly:

Get up. Beatrice, get up! Up, Beatrice, get up!

Slowly she returns to the chair. He lays wood by grate, moves to lay blanket over her legs again.

'Ye hasten to the dead? What seek ye there?' Do you know those lines? Shelley! 'Ye hasten to the dead, what seek ye there?'

Lays, then lights the fire.

Do you know I hardly know the sound of your voice? Is it shrill? Mellow? Thin? I used to sit in buses or trains and gaze at beautiful girls, and sometimes they'd smile at me and I'd smile back and imagine every virtue in their faces: gentleness, understanding, passion. And then they'd speak and everything I'd imagined about them would shatter. How can lovely eyes have ugly voices I wonder? Is your soul on your lips or in your eyes? Answer me that. Just that. Say 'eyes', or 'lips' say. Or point. Do that, even. Just point. Not even that? Ah, well.

Listen to the wood crackling. Smell it?

She breathes in.

Again. Can you do it again?

She turns away. For his foolish persistence she has, for the moment, dismissed him, as though he understands nothing.

You think I don't understand, don't you? How I recognise that look. The female dismissing the male. Don't you see pain in *my* eyes? Do you imagine I'd bring you here, commit a whole year to you if I understood nothing? Do you?

Silence.

Impatiently ADAM leaves her, wanders around the kitchen. Turns on oven. Sound of hissing.

There's even gas!

Turns on tap.

And water, too!

We've got fire and water. Miracles!

He picks up the other blanket, sits in a chair, tucks the blanket round his legs, like her.

Aren't they? Miracles!

There is a long pause as the two sit.

The days are passing, the weeks, even.

PART 2

Morning.

ADAM rises abruptly from the chair and throws his blanket down.

ADAM Gentleness is no good, I can see that. Just produces more self-pity doesn't it? Look at you. Your face is falling apart with self-pity. You don't impress me with your silence. I could do that, what you're doing, sitting there, silent, morbid, lifeless. I could do that. You're even enjoying it aren't you? How lovely it is, suffering! All the world is against you, isn't it? Eh? All the world is a fool, and you're alone, suffering! (*Mocking.*) 'I'm alone, alone. We're all born alone.' Lovely! Splendid! Very satisfying. Suffering. Lovely, lovely suffering.

Regrets outburst.

And yet…why should I mock you? I know. You were right to dismiss me. We don't really know each other yet. Poor girl! Grieve for ourselves, don't we? But look!

Reaches for brass pan on mantelshelf.

I'll polish old brass!

Moves to where the window was broken.

I'll repair windows! I'll live, go on! (*Pause.*) You don't believe me do you? She doesn't believe me.

Writes this in dust on a piece of furniture.

She – doesn't – believe – me.

Pretends to hear this next question as though from outside front door. Cups his ear.

Eh? What's that? *Why* doesn't she believe me? Why?

Opens door. Cold wind. Shouts answer into it.

Because you never recover! That's why! Never!

Turns back to BEATRICE, door still open.

Why don't we ever recover, Beatrice? Won't you answer that, even? Not even that. Poor Beatrice. I mean it. Poor, poor Beatrice. 'Poor Adam' do I hear you say?

He looks outside.

What colour is the wind do you think?

No response. Closes door. Leans against it, defeated.

Perhaps we should wait for the winter to pass.

Each is living in their hell.

The days are passing, the weeks, even.

PART 3

Late evening. ADAM singing.

ADAM   'The wind doth blow tonight, my love,
          And a few small drops of rain,
          I never had but one true love,
          In cold grave she was lain.'

     He recites the rest.

'I'll do as much for my true love
As any young man may;
I'll sit and mourn all at her grave
For a twelvemonth and a day.'

See, even *I've* become morbid. If we stay together
many more months do you think we'll just fall apart?
Disintegrate with misery? Waste away? Look, if I sit
here and you there, day after day, quite still, do you
think God would take pity and turn us to stone for
ever and ever?

Let's try. You there, me – here. Quite still. Don't
move now.

     They freeze for a long, long time. Then:

Have you ever known a God as un-obliging as ours?

     *BEATRICE smiles. ADAM catches her. Moves quickly
     to face her.*

You smiled. I caught you smiling. Don't deny it. For
that – a present. Today – a special treat.

     *ADAM looks around till he finds a hairbrush. Stands
     behind BEATRICE, unpins her hair to release a rich
     mane. Then brushes. Firm, caressing.*

See what we give to the people we comfort? The
tested gestures of love, what we know has given
pleasure before. Does that offend you? But what's
the alternative? Immobility? Silence? I used to
remain silent because it seemed to me that all my
thoughts should be kept for one person only. To

know more than one person was to betray them, I
thought.

That's what made my wife miserable, my silence.
More than anything else. But what could I tell
her? Every ounce of passion was claimed, given
elsewhere.

She had her retribution, though, my wife. One day
a young man came from another country to be our
guest. He had eyes like an uncertain child in a festive
room and he laughed with pleasure at everything he
saw. And gradually – I watched her – gradually my
wife unfolded from her misery. It was her turn. She
gathered the tested gestures of *our* love, revealed the
secret corners of *our* past. They held hands, walked
over *our* bridges, looked into *our* rivers, ate in *our*
friendly restaurants, and were kind to one another.

For two weeks she blossomed as she once did.
Every ounce of *her* passion was now claimed, given
elsewhere. And as I lay in bed till the early hours,
waiting for her return, no one at my side, imagining
the tenderness and passions they were sharing
then, just then, at that precise and very moment
– I clenched my teeth and cried 'justice' to myself.
Justice, justice, justice!

To know more than one person *is* to betray them.

But – who remains silent for ever?

You have lovely hair.

He moves to kneel in front of her.

Beatrice, you have lovely hands, and eyes, and lips,
and skin. Do you forgive me for saying it? You don't
know what it means to be able to say those things
to a woman. You only know that a woman needs
to hear them said but you don't know the pain that
grows in a man who is struck dumb with no one to
say them to, you don't know that do you?

No, I will *not* touch you, but will you let me look at
you?

For the first time a stirring in BEATRICE's eyes; a struggle with herself. Should she respond or not?

ADAM sees the hesitation, risks a movement: lays his head in her lap.

Do you think the winter will ever pass?

Closes his eyes.

Very slowly, costing her effort, BEATRICE raises her arm, and gently lays her hand on his head. As she does so an enormous tension is released from her. She can relax. Grateful, she closes her eyes.

SPRING

PART 4

Morning.

A long ray of sunshine cuts through the room.

BEATRICE opens her eyes. Is startled, then realises where she is.

Gently she raises ADAM's head, takes her blanket to cushion him where her lap was, slides off her chair, and moves out of the house.

In her absence the sunlight grows stronger. The room is witness to winter passing.

She returns, in her hands a large bunch of primroses. Lays them upon the still-sleeping ADAM till he is decorated from head to foot.

On the last flower he awakes.

ADAM I've not had such a beautiful thing done to me since –

BEATRICE See what we give to the people we comfort?

ADAM thrills to her voice but she warns:

The *tested* gestures of love!

ADAM   You garlanded your lover with primroses?

BEATRICE   Every morning!

ADAM   And at night?

BEATRICE   Oiled my skin with a different scent.

ADAM   Lucky man.

BEATRICE   (*Contemptuous.*) Lucky?

ADAM   Some women make their lovers wait –

BEATRICE   Loved!

ADAM   – offer love like a favour.

BEATRICE   Your sluts and whores do that. Not real women.

ADAM   Then you're a rare woman. Now what is it?

BEATRICE   So many people considered me a 'rare woman'.

ADAM   Aren't you? You seem so sure, so confident. Look at
              you. Proud head, penetrating eyes. Sad, weary but
              penetrating.

BEATRICE   (*Small laugh.*) Aren't you intimidated?

ADAM   Of course! I feel I want to rush away and change my
              clothes, they're all wrong and ill shaped. The clothes
              I have belong to an estate agent. You make me feel
              clumsy and careless. Of course I'm intimidated. You
              are a rare woman.

              Again she turns her face away.

              Please. Don't return to silence.

BEATRICE   You must not –

ADAM   Must not what?

BEATRICE   You must not –

ADAM   What? What? What must I not?

BEATRICE   Gently, Adam, gently. You must allow me –

ADAM   – all the world! All the world I'll allow you. How can
              I refuse you? Look at that sun, look at that day! It's
              a day for offerings. All the world I'll offer you, only
              ask. Just ask.

My mother used to ask me, 'Do you love me?' and
I'd say, 'Yes!' And then she'd say 'How much?' And
I'd say, 'Ten pence.' And she'd say, 'Is that all?' And
I'd say, 'Fifty pence.' 'No more?' she'd ask. And I'd
say 'All the world, then. I love you all the world, all
the world, all the world.'

What more can I offer you? Ten-pence for a cup of
tea? The cream off the milk? I give it you, and the
sun and this whole day.

BEATRICE You'll drown me with words.

ADAM Do I embarrass you?

BEATRICE No.

ADAM Overwhelm you?

BEATRICE No.

ADAM Then thank God for me and stop complaining
– that's the way I feel. After a winter of silence that's
the way I feel. Stop complaining!

> *Sound of a crash from outside. ADAM investigates.*
> *Returns with a fallen drainpipe and some broken*
> *tree branches.*

Spring comes and it's time to repair the damages of
winter.

> *Looks round the room and, on seeing a broken*
> *hatstand, places the drainpipe over it and puts the*
> *branches into the drainpipe. There is now a 'tree' in*
> *the room which, when the walls later move aside,*
> *becomes a tree in the country scene.*

I am *so* hungry.

> *BEATRICE goes the oven and from it with oven cloths*
> *retrieves a 'cooked meal'.*

You made it. Lasagne. I just happened to say I like it
and you made it.

BEATRICE (*Irony.*) Your command is my wish.

ADAM   I see. It's to be like that is it? I'm always suspicious of a woman's supplication. Still, I'll risk it. Even again! (*Smells it.*) Mmm! You really *can* cook!

BEATRICE   Lasagne is hardly cooking.

ADAM   You're cheating. Supplication and false modesty.

BEATRICE   Come now, if I have false modesty you have false innocence.

ADAM   Aaaaaah!

BEATRICE   (*Apologetically.*) Did that hurt?

ADAM   Didn't you mean it to hurt?

BEATRICE   I'm sorry. Old reflexes.

ADAM   It came so easily, so quickly.

BEATRICE   Long practice. I'm sorry.

ADAM   You put me on guard.

BEATRICE   Please – don't be on guard.

> *He relents. Prepares table with a great flourish, throwing over it a dazzling white cloth. Reaches for cutlery, crockery.*

ADAM   I'm ravenous. You know, as a kid, when I was very hungry – and I was always very hungry – I'd call out 'Where's the food? I'm ravishing!'

BEATRICE   I'm afraid the village didn't have much choice of wines, there was only this.

ADAM   Most people when I tell them that story say 'you are, you are'.

BEATRICE   You are, you are.

ADAM   Didn't seem very funny this time.

BEATRICE   And these, look, there was a little antique shop, I picked them up cheaply.

ADAM   Serviette rings! We're building a home! Silver?

BEATRICE   Georgian, too.

ADAM   You know?

BEATRICE   Quite cheap, I promise you. The poor man didn't really know what they were.

ADAM   So of course you had to buy serviettes.

BEATRICE   (*Producing them.*) Are you angry?

ADAM   Angry?

BEATRICE   At my extravagance?

ADAM   Stop apologising. We're building a home. White linen! It'll be a royal meal.

BEATRICE   And forgive me, this material, I thought I'd make curtains, golden, for the summer.

ADAM   It's beautiful.

BEATRICE   And I found this pullover. I thought it might suit you. Do you like it? You don't think it presumptuous? I'm sorry if you –

ADAM   Please, please, I can't bear you being apologetic all the time. You knew it would suit me.

BEATRICE   I'm not always sure about people, not everyone likes things chosen for them.

ADAM   Not everyone likes another's choice to be so right. (*Testing her.*) What colour should we paint these walls?

BEATRICE   White.

ADAM   And what should be the colour of the furniture?

BEATRICE   Golden.

ADAM   You're so sure.

BEATRICE   Like the curtains.

ADAM   You answer so quickly.

BEATRICE   (*Desperate to dismiss it.*) A minor talent.

> *Nevertheless, he regards her with a mixture of admiration and caution.*
>
> *Ceremoniously he pulls out a chair for her. She mistakes his movement, and flinches.*

ADAM   No, I won't touch you. Won't you sit, ma'am?

She does. He uncorks bottle.

To whom, or what, shall we drink?

BEATRICE   Perhaps we should just raise glasses and not tempt fate.

ADAM   Still afraid?

BEATRICE   Afraid? I'm neither afraid nor brave. I feel nothing. Let's just drink.

They raise glasses, and drink, slowly, remaining still when the glasses are drained.

Do you know what my husband once said to me? 'You're like a queen,' he said, 'without a country. I hate queens without their country.'

ADAM   Dangerous, that's why.

BEATRICE   *He* felt nothing and I felt nothing. We spent the last years living a cold, courteous lie.

ADAM   But your lover?

BEATRICE   Ah, he was a leader of men.

ADAM   He was or you wanted him to be?

BEATRICE   That's just what he would have asked.

ADAM   Then I know him and I know you and I know all that passed between you.

She seems oblivious to him and what he says. Possessed by memories she storms angrily ahead hardly caring whether he hears her or not.

BEATRICE   What I can't forgive is that he made me feel indifference. I can't bear indifference. I despise the man who makes me feel indifference.

ADAM   Beatrice –

BEATRICE   Despise him!

ADAM   Beatrice!

BEATRICE   From my husband I expected no more, but from him –

ADAM   You're not talking to *me*, Beatrice –

BEATRICE   From him – to spit at the devotion I chose to give
            him.

ADAM   You're not talking to *me*.

BEATRICE   He'll find no one, no one to give him so much.

ADAM   BEATRICE!

BEATRICE   No matter where he searches or for how long, no
            one!

            ADAM rises and begins to clear away.

            I'm sorry.

ADAM   I've bought some paint. We must paint the house.

BEATRICE   I'm a bore aren't I!

ADAM   From top to bottom – we must paint the house
            from top to bottom if we intend to live the year out
            together.

BEATRICE   You're so gentle and I'm such a bore. I didn't mean
            to hurt you.

ADAM   We'll greet the summer with those white walls.

BEATRICE   I don't ever mean to hurt anyone, forgive me.

ADAM   We'll greet the summer with white walls and golden
            curtains.

BEATRICE   I'll look in the shop for bits and pieces. Nothing
            expensive.

ADAM   What more can I do? I don't know what more I can
            do. Everything explodes.

BEATRICE   I promise, promise.

ADAM   I have a desperate need to give joy, Beatrice, create
            laughter, heal someone.

BEATRICE   And I need to be healed. I've destroyed a marriage
            and failed a lover – I need to be healed!

            Long silence.

ADAM   We must stop this – encouraging each other's misery. Let's see how long we can stay away from morbidity. Can you use a paintbrush?

BEATRICE   (*Curtsying, play-acting.*) I can try, my lord.

ADAM   Your 'lord'?

BEATRICE   Yes.

ADAM   Really, really your 'lord'?

BEATRICE   Really, really.

ADAM   Then take this brush.

> *Reaches for pail of whitewash, brushes and two white aprons.*

And wear this.

> *Aprons on, brushes in hand, each turns a different way, looking for the first wall.*

This one?

BEATRICE   No, that one.

ADAM   (*After the merest pause.*) That one, then.

> *They attack the wall.*

(*Reciting.*) 'When I was a windy boy and a bit
And the black spit of the chapel fold…'

BEATRICE   You recite.

ADAM   '…Sighed the old ramrod, dying of women'.

BEATRICE   You sing.

ADAM   'I tiptoed shy in the gooseberry wood
The rude owl cried like a tell-tale tit,
I skipped in a blush as the big girls rolled
Ninepin down on the donkey's common
And on seesaw Sunday nights I wooed
Whoever I would with my wicked eyes.'

BEATRICE   What else do you do?

ADAM   Dance.

BEATRICE   And?

ADAM   Weave large tapestries.

BEATRICE   Full of fantasies?

ADAM   (*Mock surprise.*) How did you know?

BEATRICE   How much I know about you already!

ADAM   And you?

BEATRICE   I? Oh, none of those things. (*Pause.*) Men come to me with ideas, politicians with doubts, poets seek my praise. My home is filled with people who trust my instinct: which woman for the right man; the correct meal for a gathering; the strength of an argument. But for myself? In my little finger I have energy to shape so much, and yet – I flutter from one grand scheme to the next and settle my mind nowhere.

ADAM   Sing. You must be able to sing.

BEATRICE   Not even that. I thought I could till my voice rasped back at me through a tape recorder. Somehow I can't seem to make the notes happen. A moan comes out, a gurgle, a sort of gasping for air.

ADAM   I don't believe you. Everybody can sing. I've never heard of anyone not being able to sing. Why, it must have been the first sound of the first man.

BEATRICE   Never! The first man gave a long wail and ran round and round in terror.

ADAM   Wrong!

BEATRICE   The first sound was a wail. The most nerve-racking sound in the world.

ADAM   Wrong!

BEATRICE   There was his wife and there were his children – and he ran, wailing.

ADAM   Wrong! It wasn't a wail at all, it was a cry of joy, a great leap in the air.

BEATRICE   Ran! A long, long way away.

ADAM   It only *seemed* as though he ran a long way because he got lost in the excitement of being alive.

BEATRICE   (*Smiling.*) You don't really believe that do you,
           Adam?

ADAM   If I teach you to sing will you believe me?

BEATRICE   It just isn't possible, I know.

ADAM   If I give your throat a dozen notes will you believe
       me?

BEATRICE   You're very sweet, but –

ADAM   Will you?

BEATRICE   I –

ADAM   Will you?

> *She is resigned. He hums a melodic scale.*

Try that.

> *A dry, awful complaint comes from her throat.*

BEATRICE   I must be mad. Adam, believe me. I feel
           embarrassed.

ADAM   You didn't listen. To produce a sound like that you
       couldn't have listened.

BEATRICE   I listened, believe me, I heard you but I just couldn't
           repeat it.

ADAM   Again.

> *He hums the same scale.*

BEATRICE   Please don't make me.

ADAM   Again.

> *He hums. She tries, and again a strange, guttural
> sound comes from her throat.*

But you're not listening – everybody sings.

BEATRICE   I'll cry, if you go on I'll cry.

ADAM   It's like not having eyes, or being lame. What do you
       do with babies if you can't lullaby them?

BEATRICE   I can't I can't, that's it, I can't. No sound, I make no
           sounds, just a long moan, or a silence. I destroyed

a marriage and failed a lover now leave me alone, damn you, leave me alone.

ADAM (*Realises he's gone too far.*) Hush, then, I'm sorry.

BEATRICE Well I can't, I just can't sing.

ADAM I'm sorry.

BEATRICE I never could.

ADAM Hush.

BEATRICE You think I haven't tried? I've tried and I've tried, I just can't.

ADAM I'm sorry. My God, is there nothing we touch that doesn't explode?

BEATRICE Nothing!

There was nothing he or I could touch either that didn't explode. What battles we fought. I thought I saw 'God' in him but we fought. The boy with wings! I used to sit at his feet, literally, curled on the floor, hugging him. 'Get up,' he'd say, he hated it. 'Get up, off your knees, no woman should be on her knees to a man.' He never believed he was worth such devotion. It embarrassed him.

And I was dead, a piece of nothing until he touched me, or spoke to me, or looked at me. Even his look was an embrace. I used to nag him for all his thoughts, hungry for everything that passed through his mind, jealous that he might be thinking something he couldn't share with me. I couldn't take my eyes off him. I knew every curve, every movement his features made. I don't know why we fought.

That's a lie. I knew very well why we fought. Exclusivity! I couldn't bear to see the shadow of another person fall on him. Even hearing him talk to someone else on the phone about 'ways to mend the world' was enough to make prickles of the hair on my neck. How dare he think *my* intellect was not enough to set to right his silly world's intolerable pain! Do you know what I used to do? Sneer! I used to sneer and denigrate anyone who was near and dear to him – friends, relatives, colleagues. Even his children, I couldn't bear the demands they made on him. When they were desperately ill I dismissed their complaints as childish maladies, and when they cried because their father constantly stayed away I accused them of artfulness. No one missed the whip of my sneers.

But – he was a leader of men, and leaders of men fight back. Every word became a sword, a bomb destroying nerve centres, crippling the heart. We hurled anything at each other: truths, lies, half-truths, what did it matter as long as it was poison, as long as we gave each other no peace. Sometimes he would give in, for love of me, and when the next battle came round I would taunt him with his previous surrender. And when he didn't surrender I would accuse him of being afraid of his wife. No peace, none at all, neither for him nor myself.

Human communication difficult? Not for us it wasn't. We communicated only too well. In the end – we were demented. And for what? A love so desperate that we fought for it not to be recognised, terrified that we might reveal to each other how helpless we were. Isn't that madness? That's madness for you, since without love I've neither appetite nor desire. I'm capable of nothing. And I haven't the strength to forgive myself.

There, can you still teach me to sing? Teach me to love myself better – then perhaps I'll sing.

ADAM returns to the painting. BEATRICE watches him.

How patient you are.

She takes up painting again, kneeling. Both continue in silence.

Softly ADAM sings the song he sang in winter.

BEATRICE struggles to join him. Both are trying to ease her tension.

Soon, they hum together, she slightly off-key.

He hears her, moves towards her, encouraging her singing. She continues kneeling, struggling to sing.

Then:

Close your eyes.

ADAM obeys.

BEATRICE rises, moves to him, unbuttons her blouse then his shirt and, for the first time, they touch – cheek to cheek, bare breast to breast.

No passionate embrace, but – passion!

Nothing should be held back, ever. We're mean, Adam, we're all so mean, nothing should ever be held back.

He holds her away to look into her face. She turns from him.

ADAM   You're blushing.

BEATRICE   Don't look at me.

ADAM   Like a young girl, you're blushing.

BEATRICE   Please, just hold me, don't look at me.

ADAM   Why? I want to look at you. Lift your head, Beatrice, look at me. Don't turn away, face me.

She falls to her knees trying to escape his look.

From the old chest he withdraws the cloth she bought for the curtains. Shrouds her with it and raises her to her feet.

(*Quoting her.*) 'No woman should be on her knees to a man!'

He goes outside and shouts back.

And then we'll whitewash the outside walls, paint the window frames… You'll see! We'll paint ourselves a white temple. You hear me? Xanadu! A stately pleasure dome decreed. I'll worship you in it! You hear? Xanadu! Stately pleasure dome! White temple!

Returns. Takes her in his arms.

To worship you in!

A white light burns the scene.

END OF ACT ONE

Act Two

SUMMER

PART 5

A new morning.

All is changed. White walls, furniture newly covered in golden material complementing the curtains that deck the windows.

BEATRICE, dressed in a beautiful yellow garment, enters newborn into the world.

She is in love with the room, the morning, herself. Stands before a mirror, and stretches her limbs long and sensuously.

Embarrassed, she turns away laughing, girlishly. In this mood she wanders round the room touching its many textures.

ADAM enters, watches her. It's some seconds before she notices him. They approach one another. She feels the shape of his body, remembering.

He is about to speak. She gestures him not to. She wants only to look at him, with incredulity, disbelieving her good fortune.

Pulls him gently here, there, to see him in different lights. Wanders away, turning swiftly every so often, fearful he might not be there.

At a certain moment the walls and furniture move leaving only the 'tree' and a bright summer sun. They are out in the fields.

BEATRICE, still girlish, tucks her dress into her pants while ADAM bends to touch his toes. Leapfrog! With a great 'whoop' she leaps over his back, then he over hers.

They walk, lovers breathing the air, drinking each other's presence, delighting in their bodies which we guess have been brought alive again.

Soon they lie down – on a bank.

A zany mood afflicts them.

ADAM   Look at that bird, that one there, the one that just seems to be hanging in the air. Do you believe it?

BEATRICE   Believe it?

ADAM   Believe in it.

BEATRICE   In its existence?

ADAM   No, no. Not its existence. I mean – well – look at it. You can't really believe it can stay in the air just by flapping about like that, can you?

BEATRICE   What keeps it in the air then?

ADAM   God knows! Lots of other birds blowing upwards, I think.

BEATRICE   Like aeroplanes.

ADAM   Like aeroplanes! All that metal in the air. All that metal and all those people suspended in air, with nothing underneath them.

BEATRICE   Except air.

ADAM   Except air.

BEATRICE   And friends blowing up!

ADAM   What about ships! Silly isn't it? That mass of iron and wood –

BEATRICE   – and people –

ADAM   – and people, all floating –

BEATRICE   – with nothing underneath them –

ADAM   – except frogmen –

BEATRICE   – thousands of them –

ADAM   – swimming with one arm and holding up the boat with the other.

BEATRICE   And clouds.

ADAM   And clouds?

BEATRICE   Making all that noise, thunder. At least so they say.

ADAM   Oh that one. I've never believed that one.

BEATRICE I mean what's in a cloud? Mist! Nothing!

ADAM   And those flowers.

BEATRICE Which ones?

ADAM points.

They're not flowers, they're Windberries. I'll make
you a Windberry tart.

ADAM   All those colours, all those patterns – you know what
they say about those don't you?

BEATRICE What?

ADAM   That they – you won't believe this – that they come
from a tiny seed, no bigger than this. All those
colours look! No bigger than this.

BEATRICE They tried to tell me that one at school.

ADAM   Did you believe them?

Zany mood has passed.

BEATRICE I planted forests, once, for two years, reclaiming lost
land. My father studied plants and I learned from
him the drama of watching things grow. And when
my university days were over I took to the hills and
bandaged dying firs and damaged pines.

Zany mood half returns.

Have you ever heard of the Soldanella or the Shasta
Daisy? The White Laurustinus and the Red Ice
Plant? Did you know that Convularia Majalis was
the Latin name for Lily of the Valley? 'Consider the
Convularia Majalis how they grow, they toil not,
neither do they spin; and yet I say unto you that
even Solomon in all his glory was not arrayed like
one of these.' I made things grow, Adam, once I
made things grow.

ADAM   And now?

BEATRICE Now?

She rolls over to whisper in his ear.

Now I have a golden eagle for a lover.

ADAM (*Pretending not to hear.*) What?

BEATRICE (*Still whispering.*) I have a golden eagle for a lover.

ADAM (*Still pretending.*) What?

BEATRICE (*Shouting.*) I have a golden eagle for a lover!

ADAM But the sun has burnt his poor wings.

BEATRICE Nothing shall burn – I am your sun.

ADAM Where shall I fly?

BEATRICE Anywhere – as long as I'm with you.

ADAM Aren't you my sun?

BEATRICE (*Sensual, soft-toned passion.*) When you need me to be your sun – I'm your sun. Comfort? I'll offer words. Rest? My breasts, my lips. Whatever you call for you shall have.

ADAM And you? What shall I give you?

> *She pauses for the briefest moment before deciding whether he can take what she is about to demand.*

BEATRICE Every second! Every touch, every thought, every feeling, every second – for me.

ADAM You demand?

BEATRICE You deny me the right to demand?

> *Jest or test?*
>
> *Both confront the prospect of total surrender to, and expectation from, each other. Will he commit? All his efforts seem to have led to this moment. Is she right?*
>
> *Finally:*

ADAM I deny you nothing!

> *BEATRICE leaps up. She's consumed with joy and triumph. Cups her mouth and cries out to the vast landscape.*

BEATRICE I have a golden eagle for a lover! A golden eagle for a lover!

Adam, are we ready? Let's go. Now! Test ourselves away from here. Before the winter comes let's go away from this house, these hills, these fields. This is the loveliest time. Let's go – now.

ADAM   Now?

BEATRICE   Now!

ADAM   From all this?

BEATRICE   Stay, and we tempt fate.

ADAM   Not yet. Trust me.

BEATRICE   Don't you see what's happened to me? Dear God! You've made me *feel* again. I'd like to be young for you! I'd like to be shy and pure and untouched for you. Let's go, Adam. We've had this place, this time – we've had it, all it can give. There's nothing more here. Let's go.

ADAM   Trust me.

BEATRICE   Trust you? Oh I trust everything to you. You've made me blossom. I'm opening, Adam, watch me, watch me, watch meeeeeee.

> *BEATRICE towers, stretches out to the sun.*
>
> *ADAM regards her but can't follow her.*
>
> *In this position they freeze.*
>
> *The sun sets, the walls and furniture return.*
>
> *The days are passing, the weeks, even.*

PART 6

ADAM   Two kinds of love, two kinds of women. The woman whose love embraces you, the woman whose love oppresses you. The first keeps its distance, and you emerge slowly, confidently. The second burns the air around you till you can't breathe or speak.

You know, when I was born I was born with a great laughter in me. Can you believe that? A great laughter, like a blessing. And some people loved and some people hated it. It was a sort of challenge, a test against which people measured themselves; and I could never understand the extremes of either their love or their hate.

Have you ever been with a beautiful woman, a really breathtaking beauty, and watched the passionate waves of devotion and loathing she attracts? Noticed how the people around feel the irresistible need to say sly, unpleasant things to show they're not intimidated by her beauty? So it was with my laughter.

And she, who had no need to measure herself against anything or anyone because she was endowed with her own loveliness, her own intelligence – she too began measuring herself against that laughter. And why? Because I was *born* with it, *she* hadn't bestowed it. She couldn't bear that.

She found enemies where there were none, saw betrayals in every act, broke each smile, stormed every moment of peace we'd built. And once, when I cursed her from a sickbed, when *I* lost control, then *she* became calm and took control. Only she could nurse me back to health, you see. 'You,' she said, 'are incapable.'

Soon, she made no sense. 'I see God in you,' she'd say one day, and the next pour sourness on my work. She'd rave and regret, applaud and destroy, love and devour. Mad! Mad, mad, mad woman! *Why* does a woman destroy her love with such desperate possessiveness, why? She had no need to be desperate – I *was* possessed!

And yet, despite what she is, there's a part of her doesn't deserve what she is. Through all that madness – and it *is* a madness you know, love like that, a madness – but through it all I understood her need to howl. Pain. Such a tortuous relationship. And she understood, also. In moments of peace we both understood and comforted each other. But then she'd forget and howl again, such terror in her voice, such venomous poison. And it went on and on and on and on, relentlessly, crippling us both.

Where is she now, I wonder? Lonely, for sure. Lost somewhere and lonely. No one has the right to take away laughter from a man, or deny a woman her beauty. Lonely, unutterably lonely.

And me? 'Me' rummages about the world looking for bits and pieces of old passions, past enthusiasms, echoes of old laughter. A feeble search, really. I see things wanting her to see them. I visit places wanting her to be with me. I think thoughts wanting her to share them, crying out for her praise. All that I do, everything, is a pale reflection of her taste, her vivid personality.

We never recover, do we? With her the laughter became cries of pain; without her the laughter is gone. We never really recover.

> *When BEATRICE turns to him we see she is a changed woman. The venom of her words is matched by the hardness in her eyes.*

BEATRICE You dare tell me all this?

ADAM Dare? I confided in you. Why 'dare'?

BEATRICE Not one thought should you be thinking that is not directed at me.

ADAM (*Shocked.*) Beatrice!

BEATRICE At me! Not one thought!

ADAM But I'm trusting you. With confidences I'm trusting you.

BEATRICE And I trusted you. With my love!

ADAM You've not understood.

BEATRICE My 'golden eagle'.

ADAM You can't have been listening.

BEATRICE My husband always said I expected too much from people.

ADAM I laid myself bare. You can't…

BEATRICE To make me witness to such insensitivity.

ADAM Insensitivity?

BEATRICE Such crudeness.

ADAM Did you want passionate lies?

BEATRICE Passionate lies? Is that what our time has been? Your singing, your 'poetry recitals', your declarations from the clouds? Passionate lies?

ADAM I know these battlegrounds, Beatrice, let's leave them.

BEATRICE Why? Afraid of what might be said, my brave hero, my 'golden eagle'?

ADAM Let's be wise, recognise familiar warnings.

> *ADAM retreats from her by taking up a drawing pad, a scene through the window.*

BEATRICE Familiar to us both!

ADAM To us both. Be generous, then. I listened to your 'laments', now be generous, listen to my fears. Look at you, you're shaking with rage, you're not even listening.

BEATRICE I hear every word.

ADAM You hear what you want to hear.

BEATRICE I understand everything.

ADAM You understand what you need to understand.

BEATRICE (*Mocking.*) You see things wanting her to see them, you think thoughts wanting her to share them. Face me!

ADAM You're right –

BEATRICE Face me!

ADAM I've made a mistake –

BEATRICE Face me!

ADAM stops. Turns to face her. Attempts to make peace.

ADAM   I was insensitive. I'm sorry. Let this day pass.

BEATRICE   Oh no! You don't dismiss me like that. I have a right to be answered.

ADAM   Rights! Rights! We now demand rights?

BEATRICE   (*Suddenly understanding.*) You're afraid.

ADAM   A growing tree blots out the sun.

BEATRICE   I reached for the sun and you became afraid.

ADAM   Yes, afraid. And how well you know it.

BEATRICE   I grow and you become terrified.

ADAM   Yes, yes, terrified. Stop pretending all that innocence.

BEATRICE   You poor thing, you.

ADAM   A woman reaches for the sun, the battle-cry goes up, and the old war is declared again.

BEATRICE   You poor, pathetic thing, you.

ADAM   And I try to believe it can't be true, not all the time, but there it is – declared again!

BEATRICE   (*Witheringly.*) There's neither fight nor love in you.

ADAM   (*If only she knew.*) No love in me?

> *Pause.*

BEATRICE   Why do you draw? A professor of words – why do you dabble in shapes? You're not very good at it.

> *He attempts to ignore her.*

This strange English passion for hobbies. Don't your students love you enough? The great 'authority on Romantic Poets'? Why this need for weekend pastimes?

ADAM   How, how could I have made the same mistakes again?

BEATRICE   Poor Adam.

ADAM   You don't say 'poor Beatrice'?

BEATRICE   Why should I?

ADAM   No indeed, why should you.

They are not facing each other.

The silence is long.

BEATRICE   Adam? I'm cold.

ADAM   The leaves are falling. There's a heavy wind.

BEATRICE   I need something to keep me warm. (*Silence.*) No suggestions these days? Your lady's cold. (*Silence.*) And your silence is even colder. Adam, your poor lady is cold.

From a drawer he takes out two pullovers. One is brown, the other rust.

The brown one he puts on himself, the other he pulls down over BEATRICE.

They are now dressed in autumnal colours, green, golden, brown and rust.

Why don't *you* warm me?

He needs to, fears to, but finally takes her in his arms.

A long, long kiss.

The light changes.

The days pass, the weeks, even.

PART 7

ADAM falls limp in her arms.

BEATRICE   Adam! Oh, it's games now is it? Adam! Really, it's very boyish and charming but I'm a mature woman, games irritate me. (*She waits.*) Adam, don't weary me, please.

She lowers him to the divan. Attends to the room.

Adam, I know you want to cheer me up but I'm afraid that some of the games you play are not right for the age we have. Adam! Adam!

She moves to him, turns him over.

My God, how white your face has turned. ADAM!

Places hand on his forehead.

But there was no warning. What've you caught you foolish boy? There was no sign. Such a fever, foolish boy, such a fever.

She lays a blanket over him, pulls a small table and armchair to the bedside.

From a sideboard withdraws a bottle of brandy and glass, which she puts to ADAM's lips.

When he's drunk some she kisses him.

During her next speech the light again changes as she spends the weeks looking after him.

ADAM moves and murmurs.

She leans to him, hand caressing his face.

I'm here, my lovely one, right here. No need to cry out. Hush. Lie still, I'm here, feel me.

He settles.

She places a blanket round her shoulders awaiting his recovery.

How I wish I could sing now.

You're right, it *is* a kind of crippling when your voice can't make music. You know, I'm not really as treacherous as I sound, or cold or humourless. Sometimes a fever gets in me too and I don't know what I say. But I'm always honest, at least to myself, and good and really – very wise.

But I'm damaged. I blush for the creases in my skin. Worn limbs, second-hand. Third-hand to be precise; third-hand, bruised and damaged – I wheeze and whirr, like a clock striking the wrong hour – midnight when it's only six.

But if we'd met before meeting anyone else, then – Oh, Adam, the right hour would have struck at the right time, every time, clear and ringing. If, if, if – and what wouldn't we have done together then, eh? Raised storms among the dead, that's what we'd have done, then.

Do you know what my husband said to me? 'You're like a queen,' he said, 'without her country. I hate queens,' he said, 'without their countries.' And he was right. No home and no man to pay me homage. All my life I've looked for peace and majesty, for a man who was unafraid and generous; generous and not petty. I can't bear little men; mean, apologetic, timid men; men who mock themselves and sneer at others; who delight in downfall and dare nothing. Peace, majesty and great courage – how I've longed for these things.

He once abandoned me in a fog, that man, that man I called 'God'; in a long, London fog, left me, to walk home alone.

Peace, majesty and great courage.

And once I ran through a storm and stood on a station platform, soaking and full of tears, pleading with him to take me, take me, take me with him. And he wanted to take me, I know it, because we loved walking through streets in strange towns, discovering new shapes to the houses, breathing new airs. But he refused to show his need.

Peace, majesty and great courage – never. I've found none of these things. Such bitter disappointment. Bitter! Bitter, bitter, bitter! And out of such bitterness cruelty grows. You can't understand the cruelty that grows. And I meant none of it, not one cruel word of it. And he knew and I knew and we both knew that we knew, but the cruelty went on.

Still, 'laments' for what's done and past won't cure the invalid will they? I should be making plans for tomorrow shouldn't I? For when you get up, and the day after, and the month after, and all those long years we'll have together. What shall we do in those

years, Adam? Eh? All those great, long years ahead?
I have plans, you know, children, travel, daring all
those things you didn't dare before. We'll plot each
moment. Two brilliant lovers.

And peace, above all – peace, and trust and majesty
and all that great courage.

Get well, darling boy. My voice may not sing but my
love does. Get well.

ADAM sits up.

ADAM How long has it been?

BEATRICE The weeks have passed

ADAM What a strange fever. I've never been so ill.

BEATRICE Fatigue, tension, quite common really.

ADAM You trying to take the drama out of it? I feel sad and
weak and I'm enjoying it.

BEATRICE Enjoy it, then.

ADAM And you stayed by me all that time?

BEATRICE It sounds more heroic than it was. I suffer from
insomnia. Came easily.

ADAM If only you were always as gentle and generous.

BEATRICE Am I not? No, I'm not.

He picks up his drawing pad.

ADAM You're right, I dabble. I should be content with
words even though they're other people's words.

BEATRICE I dabble, too, which is how I recognise the dabbler.

Pause.

You don't contradict me? That's not very gallant.

ADAM You know what *I* think. You have an original mind.
Flattery's not needed from me.

BEATRICE Wrong! To believe in the nonsense of honesty?
Wrong. We all have too many failings not to need
flattery.

ADAM   So sick. I feel so thin and empty. And you stayed through the ugliness of it all.

>   *Rises, blanket over his shoulders, looks out of the window.*

The days get shorter. You can smell the days getting shorter.

>   *Pause.*

We've known each other a long time now haven't we?

>   *Both in their separate places let the blankets drop from their shoulders.*

>   *The days pass, the weeks, even.*

PART 8

>   *Preparation for the strudel.*

>   *Complete change to exuberant mood.*

ADAM   It's a long time since I've made one. Two things my grandmother bequeathed me in her will, a bagful of mint farthings and a recipe for Hungarian apple strudel.

>   *He's looking for white aprons.*

Here, you'll also need to wear one. The dust flies, I warn you.

>   *He wrings his hands like a pianist before the concert, exaggerating the movements.*

You know, my son used to say that the colour of the wind was black.

BEATRICE   That's depressing.

ADAM   No, it's positive. Black! He was certain of it, couldn't be any other colour. And he used to smile as though I must be teasing to ask a question with such an obvious answer.

BEATRICE   What colour do *you* think it is?

ADAM   Grey. The wind is grey. And now – the miracle.

BEATRICE (*Sceptically.*) The miracle! I've been waiting so long
        for this 'miracle'.

ADAM   It's magical, I promise you. Everything prepared?

BEATRICE As you asked. Sliced apples, cleaned nuts.

ADAM   The rest?

BEATRICE Raisins, caster sugar, cinnamon and olive oil.

        *BEATRICE brings these items to line on the kitchen
        sideboard.*

        *ADAM is about to make apple strudel – see appendix.
        The process is a dramatic one. The paste has been
        'resting' for twenty minutes. He will collect it from
        the kitchen.*

        *First he throws a tablecloth over the table. The
        magician prepares!*

        *He retrieves the paste from the kitchen; it lies on a
        plate, covered by a floured cloth. The paste sits like a
        round loaf. He picks it from the plate, gingerly since
        it flops about; though it should come away clean if the
        plate has been well floured.*

        He is about to lay it on the centre of the table.

ADAM   The flour! In the kitchen, quick! I left it there. For
        God's sake, the paste is drooping, quick.

        *BEATRICE hastens to find the flour. Returns. Dusts
        tablecloth.*

        *ADAM lays his paste in the centre of the cloth, reaches
        for a rolling pin, dusts that with flour, and rolls out
        paste to the first oval stage.*

        Pretty?

        BEATRICE shrugs her shoulders.

        You're a hard woman, Beatrice.

BEATRICE Hard? How short-sighted you are. I'm soft, like this
        dough, only tastier.

ADAM   You made a joke! You didn't mean to but you made a joke. First time.

BEATRICE   Your paste, attend to your paste.

ADAM   Hard! Not a bit of praise. Mean!

BEATRICE   When you've earned your praise I'll give it, lavishly. Your paste.

ADAM   Oil, hot oil, in the kitchen.

He holds out his hand like a doctor calling for the scalpel, never taking his eyes off the paste.

A sceptical BEATRICE moves off slowly.

Move, woman. Quick.

ADAM is delighted and walks round and round his paste.

Quick!

But she does move faster and brings ADAM his oil.

He pours a thimbleful over the paste, spreads it over the surface with his palm.

Ouch! It's hot. Now – (*To himself.*) – make sure it covers the surface, help it stretch, gently, and – sit, watch and wait.

Looks triumphantly at BEATRICE who again shrugs.

Hard! So hard!

BEATRICE   You delight in such small things.

ADAM   Small things? Small things? You've seen nothing yet, nothing! The miracle begins now.

And sure enough the miracle does begin now, for ADAM begins to stretch his paste and does so to the accompaniment of much gentle clowning; gentle, gentle, not frantic clowning.

Pull, my beauty, pull, pull. Stay moist, don't harden yet, stay moist.

BEATRICE impatiently rises and turns her attention to the room.

Why do you keep emptying ashtrays and tidying up?
Keep still and watch me.

BEATRICE Dirt offends me.

ADAM You can't cope with disorder can you?

BEATRICE Yes, I *can* cope with disorder, but dirt and ugliness
depress.

ADAM You're so fussy.

BEATRICE No. Fussiness belongs to pedants.

*He brings her back to the chair to ensure she is watching
before resuming work.*

ADAM A hole! Damn, a hole! Lack of practice. Still, not a
big one. Must keep my eye on that. Have to patch it
if it grows.

BEATRICE I'm sure the clowning isn't essential.

ADAM Cruel. Cruel and hard. Here, drink some milk,
soften yourself.

BEATRICE I can't bear milk. It's for women who throw javelins.
I prefer lemons.

ADAM Sour. Sour and hard. Your eyes should be growing
wider and wider, you should be astonished at my
skill.

BEATRICE I confess – it's fascinating.

ADAM How begrudgingly you say it. Damn! Another hole!
Small, it's small though. Wha hoo! Wha hoo!

*ADAM has reached the stage where he can flap the
pastry, like a sheet on a bed, to straighten it out.*

Isn't that a marvellous sight?

BEATRICE Very clever, yes.

ADAM Why – Beatrice is irritated.

BEATRICE Look, another hole, attend to your holes.

ADAM Why is Beatrice irritated?

BEATRICE She's sorry she can't share your miracle.

ADAM Of course she can. Learn, she can learn, can't she? Tomorrow *she'll* make one. (*Pause.*) She's jealous isn't she?

BEATRICE (*Contemptuously.*) Jealous!

ADAM Ha Ha! She's jealous. Pull, my beauty, pull, pull.

Did I ever tell you about my student days? About the time I nearly set fire to the kitchen I worked in? I dipped a pannier of wet chips into boiling hot fat. Don't laugh – I thought the wet chips would cool the fat down. No one ever told me cold water in hot fat ignites.

BEATRICE (*Interested despite herself.*) What happened?

ADAM It ignited!

He's pulling his pastry meanwhile.

I just stood there, watching the flames, mesmerised. And the chefs and maintenance men ran backwards and forwards screaming and trying to smother the flames with some sticky stuff and I just stood still, and everyone thought I was being calm. I ended the hero.

There, it's done. And only a few holes. Now, apples.

He strews apples along the edge of the paste.

Cinnamon.

He dusts with cinnamon.

Nuts.

He strews nuts.

Raisins.

He strews raisins.

Sugar.

He sprinkles sugar.

More cinnamon.

Dusts another coat of cinnamon.

Clean up.

> *Takes a knife and cuts away the thick edges of the paste drooping round the table.*

Now we roll.

> *ADAM clutches the left and right hand corners of the tablecloth, pulls it towards him and throws the paste and its contents forward into a roll. Continuing this movement he's able to enclose the contents of the strudel into a long pipe.*

> *When it's done he hastily drips more olive oil over the surface of the long strudel, sprinkles sugar onto the oil, cuts it into three lengths, lays three lengths onto an oven-tray, and swiftly pushes all into the oven, snapping the door shut in triumph.*

Now, tell me – why were you irritated?

BEATRICE   You were so absorbed.

ADAM   But I did it for you, to eat, to learn, to amuse you.

BEATRICE   That's how it started, perhaps. But halfway through I –

ADAM   You what? Halfway through you – ?

BEATRICE   I'm ashamed.

ADAM   Halfway through you – ?

BEATRICE   I'm so stupid and ashamed.

ADAM   You – ?

BEATRICE   I became afraid.

ADAM   Afraid?

BEATRICE   Oh don't go on. If you can't understand don't go on.

ADAM   You can't dismiss me like that – I want to understand.

BEATRICE   You just want me to say it don't you?

> *ADAM's persistent gaze drives her on.*

It's your laughter. I can't bear your laughter. It's unnatural. It casts –

ADAM   *Casts?*

BEATRICE It casts everybody out.

> *He can't believe what she's saying.*

Well me, then.

ADAM (*Incredulous.*) You resent my laughter?

BEATRICE (*Defiantly.*) Every thought, every feeling, every touch – for me.

ADAM And then there would come a moment when every touch would be flinched from, every thought sneered at and every feeling abused.

BEATRICE And that's the moment you're afraid of?

ADAM Yes.

BEATRICE (*Her turn to be incredulous.*) You think me capable of abuse?

ADAM All women.

BEATRICE But me? Me? Capable of abuse?

ADAM All women.

BEATRICE I see.

> *The tidying is done.*
>
> *They move apart.*
>
> *The days are passing, the weeks, even.*

AUTUMN

PART 9

> *Walls and furniture move.*
>
> *Dusk becomes night – a brilliant night full of stars.*
>
> *They stand, each alone, looking at the sky. A wind blows.*

BEATRICE What are you thinking?

ADAM If I said my mind's a blank, would you believe me?

BEATRICE   If you say so. (*Pause.*) Is it? (*No reply.*) Do those stars inspire only blankness?

> *ADAM still doesn't reply. Seems to be without energy.*

Why didn't you love your wife?

ADAM   Why didn't *you* love your husband?

BEATRICE   Why? There *are* no reasons. One day you just look at somebody and realise – you no longer love them. No hate, no anger –

ADAM   Just guilt! You know, I can't think of anything I've done that I haven't felt guilty for.

The first girl I ever loved was when I was twelve years old. She had a pink face and a cheeky smile and she thought she was ugly. Nothing I said persuaded her she wasn't. And so she pouted her lips and protected herself behind large, wise eyes as if she knew before love came that love was an impossible dream. For four years I wooed her until, at last, a moment came when she finally trusted herself in my arms. And in that moment, that very same moment, I betrayed her.

It happened in a camp in a valley, near one of the largest forests I'd ever seen. We went each summer, for four years, just a group of us.

And on the last summer there came a girl who took one look at me and decided – what were her own words now? She told me afterwards – she had decided from the start to 'net' me. 'Net' me! What a woman in the making she was. Tongue like a whip; will, like a great boulder; and intelligence, sharp – like a frightened hawk. And I was to carry her scars for ever, because while I wooed my childhood sweetheart this miniature adult wove her subtle net with a terrible, terrible precision.

It happened like this – vivid, so vivid, seared into memory. On the last night she, my wide-eyed sweetheart and I, at last, after four years, found the sort of exhaustion that earned us the trust of each other's arms. There we lay, among friends and the smell of wet canvas – she wasn't really in my arms but on them, and I think I kissed her cheek, once, perhaps twice, nothing more, and then she fell asleep. And as she was lying on my arm, another hand reached out for me, and – I took it.

I lie here, under these stars, and I think about camp and I remember that camp and I know, as sure as I know there's a cloud on that moon, that for that one terrible act of betrayal I have paid and wrecked my once and only life with every decision I've ever made. That's what I'm thinking.

Do you know, a friend and I once ran all the way across three fields and up a hill to see a sunset? Without stopping, all the way. Imagine that – I ran, like a lunatic, to catch a sun setting in some Cotswold hill.

How difficult it is to believe we were ever once happy.

> *Long pause.*
>
> *He tries to lighten the mood.*

Did I ever show you a photograph of one of my children? Do you know I've never shown a photograph of my children to anyone before? Always thought people who did that such a bore. Won't embarrass you will it? See the way his arms fold? Defiant! That's him! Stubborn, defiant and in charge.

BEATRICE But what is it pasted to? A Christmas card? Of your son?

ADAM (*Sensing danger.*) It's a Christmas card of a child.

BEATRICE He actually sent a Christmas card with a photograph of his son on it. What bad taste. I blush for you.

ADAM I sent it because it's a good photograph of a child, not because it's my son.

BEATRICE Like a politician endearing himself to the public. You
          have children like possessions don't you? Did you
          show it to your mistress? Every time you made love?
          Did you? Take it out and sigh over it, to show how
          guilty you felt? Did you talk about your wife in bed?
          Say how good she really was? Did you? Did you tell
          your other mistress the story of the girl at camp, the
          one with the 'large wise-eyes'? Did you? Did you?
          DID YOU?

ADAM   You're possessed aren't you? Something moves in
          you that you can't control. Can't you hear yourself?
          Don't you ever feel ashamed? The same, always the
          same sneers, always the same mockeries and sneers.
          All my life I've looked for a woman who had passion
          without deceits, wisdom without cruelty, pity without
          abuse.

BEATRICE A Christmas card of your son!

ADAM   You've not heard.

BEATRICE I think I see you now.

ADAM   Not one word have you heard.

BEATRICE Go home to your wife. She'll forgive you.

ADAM   You don't hear and you don't understand that you're
          not hearing.

BEATRICE There's nothing more you can do here.

ADAM   You've never dared have a child, have you?

BEATRICE No man with any sensitivity would have said that.

ADAM   You make up the rules as you go along.

BEATRICE My 'golden eagle'. His son on a Christmas card!

ADAM   It wasn't love you needed was it? Was it? I don't
          think you're capable of love are you? Eh? Capable
          of it? Are you? Capable of real love?

BEATRICE Yes!

ADAM   Really capable?

BEATRICE Yes, yes!

ADAM   Really, really?

BEATRICE   Yes, yes. Love. Real love. I – CAN – LOVE.

ADAM   How loudly you need to declare it.

BEATRICE   I – can – love. I – have – loved. Always. And look
           what comes back – the pathetic smell of guilt. I – can
           – love!

ADAM   The *sounds* you make, I know you make the sounds,
           the sounds and gestures of love. But feelings?
           Nothing!

BEATRICE   My dear, you're not the best person to talk about
           feelings are you? Ah, those nights at camp with
           – what was it? The 'smell of wet canvas'?

ADAM   Nothing, nothing can be trusted with you.

BEATRICE   And this other woman, 'tongue like a whip', the one
           whose scars you carry for ever?

ADAM   I confided what was precious to me.

BEATRICE   Confided?

ADAM   What you needed I gave you and it was precious to
           me.

BEATRICE   You? You were never big enough to give me what I
           needed. But I'll survive.

ADAM   Won't you just!

BEATRICE   I've more guts and passion than the three of you
           together. I'll survive.

ADAM   Won't you, won't you just!

BEATRICE   I warned you. I begged you to come away from this
           place.

ADAM   *That's* the reason?

BEATRICE   Now go home.

ADAM   Because I didn't fly off with you?

BEATRICE   You couldn't keep one mistress, give this one up. Go
           home.

ADAM   Because you couldn't wait to bring back the spoils?

BEATRICE (*Mocking.*) You see things wanting her to see them, you think thoughts wanting her to share them – go home!

ADAM You failed two men and now you need to show that it wasn't your fault.

BEATRICE Who can't be trusted with confessions, who?

ADAM Oh, you're righteous about betrayal now are you?

BEATRICE You dare throw back at me what I confided in you?

ADAM You drag dirt from me.

BEATRICE Go home to your comforts.

ADAM You oppress me.

BEATRICE To your wife, go home.

ADAM You dry up the air around me.

BEATRICE To your grinning brats – go, go.

> *ADAM slaps her face.*

You dare lift your hands to me? You dare?

> *She raises her hands to return the slap but he holds her wrists.*

ADAM Nothing touches you. You devour! Devour, devour, devour!

BEATRICE I despise you. Go home.

> *He releases her.*
>
> *Walls and furniture return.*
>
> *The days pass, the weeks, even.*

PART 10

> *BEATRICE creeps to a corner of the room, retreating once more into misery and tears.*

BEATRICE I saw God in you.

ADAM You saw in me what you wanted to see in me.

> *She's crying.*

    You cry for yourself.

BEATRICE I cry for you.

ADAM For your own misery.

BEATRICE For you, for you. I cry for you.

ADAM I believe neither you nor your tears.

BEATRICE Couldn't you see I whipped you from fear?

ADAM Couldn't you see I retreated from fear?

BEATRICE I don't know what I say.

ADAM You know everything you say, only too well, everything.

BEATRICE I'm so vulnerable and frightened.

ADAM Frightened? You?

BEATRICE Help me.

ADAM I cannot.

BEATRICE I give you my hand. Help me.

ADAM I cannot.

BEATRICE Let's make up. Like children. Let's do something silly. Climb a tree with me. Look at the moon with me. Like children, let's make up.

ADAM If only I could. You know how to tempt me, don't you? Like children, make up, if only I could.

BEATRICE Like children, Adam, a pact, like children.

ADAM And then would come another moment and it would be as though no pact had ever existed and you would spit and spit and spit again, and then you would ask to be comforted and then again you'd spit and I'd be tossed from the right hand of your passion to the left hand of your venom and I cannot, I cannot, I cannot.

BEATRICE Help me.

ADAM I cannot.

BEATRICE utters a terrifying moan that begins like a wail of despair but rises to a cry of anger – as though halfway through her wail she realises it will have no effect, that her plea will be unanswered. The cry ends abruptly.

Both realise the year has ended.

PART 11

Next day. Open cases. Each is packing. Each sips brandy.

ADAM sadly resigned.

BEATRICE chillingly calm.

BEATRICE   You know, there was nothing between us really, was there?

ADAM   (*Not asking, accepting.*) Wasn't there?

BEATRICE   We weren't even really friends, were we?

ADAM   No?

BEATRICE   My husband always told me I expected too much from people.

ADAM knows the ploy.

ADAM   (*Bitterly.*) What more?

BEATRICE   More? What more *is* there? Nothing happened. It was all play-acting. A girlish dream. I'm surprised at myself that I can still have girlish dreams. Nothing, nothing at all happened. Nothing.

ADAM   No of course not, it *was* foolishness, wasn't it! It's always foolish to try and know more than one person. To know more than one person is to betray them.

BEATRICE   On the contrary, to know only one person is to betray the world.

ADAM   Ah, yes. 'The world'!

BEATRICE   You can never be an island, you know.

ADAM Oh? Do you think when the millennium comes there won't be lovers who grow weary of their sad girls, or that wives won't weep over empty beds? Even when Jerusalem is built friends will grow apart and mothers will mourn their sons growing old.

You want me to feel for starving children? I feel for them. You want me to protest at wars that go on in the mountains? I protest. But the heart has its private aches. You must allow the heart its private aches. Not all the good great causes in this world can stop me crying for a passing love.

Long pause.

They need to comfort, forgive one another. Somehow.

Your lover, tell me, what do you remember most about him?

BEATRICE What do I remember?

A long drive into the autumn countryside I remember. The astonishment we shared that trees and fields could burn with such colours. The tremendous blaze of dying hedges, the smouldering leaves. The discovery of these things.

And you? What do you remember about her?

ADAM Moments of music, silence, adoration. I remember the scrupulous care she gave to everything she did for me – wrapping a present, cooking a meal, the attention of her eyes. And I remember cruelty – her cruelty and my cruelty.

BEATRICE I remember our plots against indifference, the easy way we picked up each other's thoughts in our 'battles with the world', the language we gave each other, my gratitude for his presence, my helplessness.

ADAM I remember that we weren't afraid to dance when we couldn't, to say we didn't know things we should have known, admit wrongs against the other.

BEATRICE   I remember that we weren't afraid to laugh
hysterically or play with children or grow old. I
remember we just weren't afraid. And I remember
when my father died in a far-off country I didn't go
to his side because I wanted to stay with my lover.
My father died alone. I was his favourite child.

ADAM   And I remember *my* father dying and my holding
his head in my hands and crying: 'Keep breathing,
Joe, come on, don't give up, don't stop, Joe.' And
my mother through her tears saying, 'You think he'll
listen to you?' and smiling, and both of us sobbing
and smiling.

They exchange smiles.

BEATRICE   Why do we remember these things I wonder?

ADAM   Oh, I don't know. Perhaps because such moments
remind us time passes, and time passing reminds us
of sadness, waste, neglect, suffering…all those lovely
moments of youth…never to return, and –

BEATRICE   – and remembering makes us gentler people?

ADAM   Perhaps. It's easier to forgive and hope to be
forgiven.

They drink on in silence for a while.

BEATRICE   I'm feeling cold. I think I have an illness coming on.

ADAM   Cold? Shall we try and warm ourselves?

He moves to the fire-grate.

These dead leaves you swept up this morning – I'll
start a fire with them.

BEATRICE   I don't know why I should be so cold.

ADAM   Soon be warm.

He tries to light the leaves. They only smoulder.

Damp.

BEATRICE   Autumn leaves. Dead. What did you expect?

*ADAM blows hard attempting to bring them to
flame.*

ADAM Burn, damn you, burn! (*Pause.*) They won't light.

> *ADAM watches the feeble smoking of autumn leaves, which refuse to ignite.*

> *BEATRICE folds and folds and meticulously folds.*

END

Appendix

THE APPLE STRUDEL

The process of making apple strudel is a dramatic one involving patience and experience. Actors learn to fence – why not to cook?

The skill of it lies in the pulling and stretching of the paste over a cloth covering the entire table until the paste is paper-thin and hanging over the edges. Apples, raisins, nuts, cinnamon and sugar are strewn along the length of the paste, which is rolled into a long pipe of strudel. This is done by pulling the cloth from under the paste, which you then flick forward.

The challenge is not to make holes in the pulling. Holes invariably appear and if they are small can be ignored; if they are large they need to be patched up by tearing a piece off the edge.

The movement required is amusingly balletic – the cook moves round and round the table pulling here, pulling there, not too much at a time, not too quickly, and most of the time using the back of his hand under the paste, drawing his hand towards him, rather than the fingers which would make holes. After a while the confident cook flaps the paste to straighten it out, like a bed sheet. To watch this being done is mesmerising, and the best chefs clown while they do it.

When the paste has been stretched until the edges are hanging over four sides of the table, the chef must move swiftly, or the paste, being so thin, will dry up. Obviously the thinner the paste becomes the more tense everyone is.

The paste is made of 1½ lbs. flour, ¾ pt. water, a pinch of salt, one egg and two teaspoonfuls of olive oil. It must be pummelled for a long time – in an automatic beater – until the mixture is smooth and pliable, just short of being tacky. The longer it is beaten the easier it is to stretch. It is left to rest for about twenty minutes and then rolled out with a rolling pin into an oval shape about 18 ins. by 9 ins., a quarter of an inch thick. Next a film of hot olive oil is rubbed gently over the entire surface and left to sink in for thirty seconds; then the pulling begins.

Little of this preparation is done in the play. The paste and ingredients are ready in time for the scene. Only the pulling and filling are acted out.

Advice should be sought from a high-class pastry-cook who would prepare the paste. It's only the pulling that Adam needs to practise and perform.

LOVE LETTERS ON BLUE PAPER

For Mike and Orna Kustow

with love for their friendship

Characters

VICTOR
A retired Yorkshire trade union official, about 65

SONIA
His wife, matronly, around 60

MAURICE
45, a professor of the history of art,
Victor's one-time protégé

T.U. OFFICIAL
30ish

Setting

A composite set in an open space: bedroom, kitchen,
lounge, a clothes line in a spacious garden, hospital
bed (out of sight until needed).

Note

All the 'love' letters (except for most of the letter
in Scene 12) must be pre-recorded by SONIA and
delivered as voiceover. It is essential they not
be delivered live. The point is to see on stage a
seemingly harsh personality but to hear someone
quite different in the voiceover. The two come
together as the play evolves.

As many speakers as possible should be placed
around the auditorium so that it seems as though
SONIA's voice is speaking gently to each member of
the audience. (See note at end.)

The world première of *Love Letters on Blue Paper* was presented by Syracuse Stage, Syracuse, USA, on 14 October 1977, directed by Arthur Storch, designed by Eldon Elder, with the following cast:

VICTOR, John Carpenter
SONIA, Myra Carter
MAURICE, Richard Clarke
T.U. OFFICIAL, Jay Devlin

Its UK première was presented by the National Theatre in the Cottesloe Theatre on 15 February 1978, directed by Arnold Wesker, designed by Bernard Culshaw, with the following cast:

VICTOR, Michael Gough
SONIA, Elizabeth Spriggs
MAURICE, Kenneth Cranham
T.U. OFFICIAL, Timothy Block

SCENE 1

Pre-set light on four, full pillows cosily puffed up on the bed.

Pre-set fades, and stage lights discover VICTOR MARSDEN sitting up in bed, patiently leaning forward while his wife, SONIA, sternly changes the last semi-starched pillowslip.

The bedroom is cluttered with paintings, sculpture and unframed canvases.

Standing by is their slightly bewildered friend, PROFESSOR MAURICE STAPLETON, just arrived, still with briefcase in his hand.

VICTOR is mischievous, fiercely intelligent.

SONIA is a large self-assured presence.

MAURICE is warm, sympathetic.

SONIA adjusts pillow behind VICTOR, slams her way to the lounge where she sits, in the shadows, by a desk, writing.

Both men come to life, talk at once, MAURICE takes off his jacket.

It is summer.

MAURICE She didn't seem to know you'd called me.

VICTOR Maurice lad! Take that chair –

MAURICE Didn't you tell her you'd called me?

VICTOR Throw those books on the floor

MAURICE She seemed so surprised to see me.

VICTOR You've chosen a good day to come.

MAURICE Why didn't you tell her you'd called me?

VICTOR Been rotten lately, not well at all.

MAURICE In fact she seemed furious to see me!

VICTOR But today! Ha! Look at that sun, wild, eh? It's gotten right into me. Full of youth. Luverly!

He breathes deeply, exaggeratedly, which forces him to cough.

Shouldn't be misled, by sunlight. Makes you want to take breaths you haven't got.

MAURICE   And why didn't you tell me you'd been ill?

VICTOR   (*Reaching for a notebook.*) You've come just at the right time –

MAURICE   I've *come*?

VICTOR   Listen to this.

MAURICE   You *called*!

VICTOR   Listen. 'The genuine creative instinct is and always has been a celebratory one. The earliest known forms of painting and ritual *may* have had to do with magic born of ignorance but – beginnings should not be mistaken for truths. Art *may* have begun in the belief that the act of mimesis contained magical properties but, *once* discovered, man looked at himself in wonderment, delighted in it, and thenceforth excelled in it only when his motivation was celebratory. *This* modest history of art will attempt to prove it.'

MAURICE   I'm impressed. It's a very good beginning. A very generous theory to want to prove. Congratulations, but first tell me why you're in bed?

Irritated, VICTOR throws book on floor ignoring the question.

VICTOR   It's rotten! Clumsy and illiterate. Like me. Written in the language of the negotiating table. Once a trade union bureaucrat always a trade union bureaucrat.

Mischievously grins, enthusiastic again.

MAURICE returns book.

But it *is* a beginning, I suppose.

MAURICE   Please, Victor, I want to talk about…

VICTOR   It won't ever be an erudite work, such as you could write, but art is celebratory and no one, not even you, Professor Maurice Stapleton, has attempted to prove why. So, old Victor, with his WEA background, his self-taught smatterings and crazy passion…

Waves arm at his bedroom exhibition.

Trouble is, no one's interested in art. Even artists have been made to feel guilty, diminishing their roles like old-fashioned sinners. 'Me, an artist? Oh no, mate, not me. I'm just ordinary, like you and him. Nothing special. I'm sure you could write *War and Peace* if you tried, or the Sonnets, or paint like Leonardo. Nothing to it, mate. All men are artists…' Cant! And if you've not got even the artists on your side, well…

VICTOR angrily pummels his cushions as if they were to blame. But his anger doesn't fit the crime. Something else must be wrong.

MAURICE gently helps put cushions in place. As he leans close to VICTOR…

I'm dying, lad.

MAURICE is paralysed.

Six months, nine months, a year. They're not certain, but soon.

VICTOR hardly notices MAURICE's shock.

Having actually said it, VICTOR turns inward and away.

Long silence, then they talk almost on top of one another.

MAURICE   I'm shattered, I can't say anything, I –

VICTOR   Aye, don't worry –

MAURICE   It's unforgivable but –

VICTOR   Nay, 'twere me, the way I told thee –

MAURICE   I mean, Victor, it's terrible –

VICTOR   Thoughtless of me.

MAURICE   Don't apologise, for Christ's sake –

VICTOR   What did I expect thee to do –

MAURICE   I just don't believe it, it's ridiculous, they've made a mistake, they always do, I mean I know of a case, cases, doctors calculate a year and patients go on and on and –

VICTOR   Maurice don't bumble! I'm dying! It's myeloid leukaemia. I waited three years for these last months and they've come and that's that. Now, let me talk.

Pause to gather strength.

Oh, I'm frightened. No doubt about that. And bitter. Look at that sun, listen to those sounds, look at those books. Who'd want to leave all that?

Picks up newspaper.

Despite all this. (*Reads.*) 'Allegations of torture to prisoners of war in North Vietnam.' Never stops does it? 'Man batters child to death. Youths batter old man to death. Quarter of London's homes without baths and heating. Sectarian killings in Belfast. Famine in India –'

Uttered in one breath which makes him cough. Irritation increases.

Still! Still, still, still! After what we did. All we did –

Long pause.

And yet – I don't want to leave any of it. I'd live with it all – just so long as I lived. (*Beat.*) Retired me from the union just in time didn't they, eh?

VICTOR gets out of bed.

MAURICE attempts to help.

VICTOR refuses. Puts on dressing-gown. Talks. While talking he takes medicine, and potters, reshuffling stacked canvases, replacing a bust. Rearranging the order of things.

I'll tell you a story. Told me by the head of one of the largest unions in West Germany. Fantastic fellow he

was, still is, I suppose. God knows! Lose touch with
them. You share a special conference or something
together, bosom pals, console each other through
dreary affairs – and you know we used to get some
boring old sods at those conferences, self-righteous
little functionaries they were – but not Heuder.
Wolfgang Heuder. Very vivid he was. Dragged into
the Wehrmacht when he was fifteen, last months of
the war. I was probably chasing him in one of my
tanks! It was him told me this story.

Seems their regiment picked up a deserter, some
poor scrawny old man who'd been out of the thing
but now they were taking in anyone who could hold
a rifle. He'd no appetite for the glorious Third Reich
right from the start so he'd precious little urgency
to die for it in its last gasps. Who would? And off
he scarpered. He could smell defeat. But – he'd no
energy. Food supplies low, footsore, wheezing – he
was caught, court-martialled, and sentenced to a
firing squad. That depressed everyone it seemed.
No one had stomach for it, not even the regiment
commander. But he was an old soak, duty was duty,
regulations was regulations. There had to be a trial,
it had to be a fair trial, there had to be a sentence, it
had to be carried out. Victims of law and order when
all law and bloody order were crumbling round
them. Madness, eh?

He switches over two paintings.

Do you like it? One of the students at The Royal
College.

Still, the Commander was an honourable man and
he asked the prisoner if he had any last wishes. You
know what the poor bugger asked for? A plate of
barley soup. Wanted to eat before dying. To go on
on a full stomach as it were. It were staple fare and
there were some left to be heated up in the kitchens
so they give it him. What he'd asked for. A plate of
barley soup!

VICTOR bends to exchange position of one bust for another, MAURICE rushes to help.

Change them over, please.

And when it were finished, now listen to this, when it were finished he asked for another plate! That were unprecedented but, nothing in the rules to say a condemned man couldn't have as much of his last request as he wanted, and rules were rules! So, another plate was called for and the man ate it slowly. And when he'd finished, yes, he asked for another plate and this time they had to wait while it was being made because they'd run out of the previous night's leftovers. And he ate! And he ate, and he ate, and he ate. Barley soup! More'n he wanted, more'n he could take. Anything so long as it delayed the moment of his death. And you know what happened? The Russians came. The sentence couldn't be carried out. Everyone fled. He lived! He couldn't have known he'd live but some instinct kept him eating. Eating to stay alive! Ha! Simple!

MAURICE's eyes are welling.

I've given you a real shock haven't I, lad? Terrible. (*Cheerfully.*) Look at those pillows. Fresh every day. She changes them. Every day. Believe it or not I get into fresh sheets every night.

Wearily climbs back into bed.

I tell her there's no need but she takes no notice. 'You spent good money on a washing machine,' she says, 'I'll use it then!' Love it, of course.

Pause.

I'm sorry, lad, you look quite pale. Daft bugger, me.

MAURICE Don't start being sorry for me, for Christ's sake! That's absurd, that's… Oh, Victor, oh Jesus, Victor! I wish at this moment I was a religious man. I wish I could tell you about an afterlife, heaven, reincarnation, something!

VICTOR   Right! That's it! What I really meant to talk about. That's why I've called you. To talk about that, afterlife, just that. But how about a cup of tea first, eh? Go to the kitchen and ask Sonia to make us some tea. Oh –

Reaches in his dressing-gown for a blue envelope. Inside a letter written on blue paper.

– and while she's doing it go into the lounge and read this. I'll have a rest meanwhile. Tire quickly these days. Only for Christ's sake don't let Sonia see you reading that letter, and don't tell her anything. She doesn't know.

MAURICE moves shakily to the door but has to sit. VICTOR laughs.

Unsteady legs? Ha, ha! I've given him unsteady legs. Ha, ha! Oh dear! I haven't learned how to be sombre all the time. Sacrilegious isn't it? Confusing!

SCENE 2

Kitchen and lounge.

MAURICE enters kitchen where he finds SONIA.

She's preparing tea-things as if she had heard.

SONIA   (*Sourly.*) What was all the laughing for?

MAURICE   Wartime stories, Sonia. He's full of them. I never tire. Victor asked me to –

SONIA   I know what Victor asked you.

He's still bewildered by her hostility.

MAURICE   I'll wait in the lounge.

SONIA doesn't bother to reply.

In lounge MAURICE sits on swivel chair by desk. Takes out letter on blue paper.

SONIA (VO)   (*Tentatively.*) I was thinking the other day. I used never to be able to call you 'darling'. Do you remember?

Lights down on lounge. As the letter is being read SONIA makes morning tea. A ritual.

While waiting for water to boil she cuts four slices of 'cut-and-come-again' cake, heats pot, counts out three teaspoonfuls of tea, pours in boiling water, covers with tea-cosy, sets out on a tray. Finally her hand rests on tea-cosy, pausing to feel the heat, then she picks up tray and moves into hall.

Over all this has been SONIA's voice continuing with the reading of the letter.

When we first met I was really plain. Plain-minded I mean, not looking. I was pretty looking but I felt daft saying 'darling' and 'sweetheart' and those things. Took about two years before I could bring myself to call you any but your name. And I only ever gave in because you bullied me. Got proper annoyed in fact. You made me say the word, forced me. Remember? I do. It was after we'd been to have tea with my grandmother. A Sunday afternoon. One of those big spreads. Everything thrown on the table, you know, from home-made pickled onions to thick old crusty rhubarb pies. And she was making her usual fuss of me. Adored me she did and I did her too, and she was teasing me and saying, 'She's a little darling, isn't she a little darling? She's my little darling.' And when we walked home you turned on me and said, 'She can say the word why can't you?' 'What word?' I asked. 'Darling!' you yelled. 'Go on, say it!' You did look funny, your face all angry while your mouth was saying words of loving. Didn't go together somehow. 'Say darling,' you shouted at me and made me giggle. And the more I giggled the more angry you got. But you won, you made me say it. (*Matter of factly.*) Darling! Sweetheart Victor, dearest Victor, darling Victor, darling, darling and my heart. I was remembering: Just today. For no reason. While I was outside cleaning the windows.

MAURICE, the letter finished, hears the rattle of tea-things, puts letter away and returns to kitchen.

He looks at SONIA, seeing a different woman. As do we.

She, however, remains indifferent. Moves to lounge. Lights down in kitchen, up in bedroom.

SCENE 3

MAURICE moves with tea tray to VICTOR's bedroom.

Rattling cups wake up a dozing VICTOR.

VICTOR   Tea! Tastes and senses. I'm really sensing everything now. When I gave up smoking all tastes came back. Now...the lot's coming back. Tastes, colours, shapes. Everything's vivid, stands out. And everything has to be special, too. Little things, like tea. Has to be the real thing, not your old tea bags. And coffee, has to be real beans, ground, none of your mean instant. And food, must have food with its own flavours. I get neurotic if cabbage tastes weedy, watery, or the lamb gets shredded like old shoelaces.

When tea is poured MAURICE returns letter.

MAURICE   Sonia?

VICTOR   Aye, Sonia.

MAURICE   Strange. All those years, almost like a second mother; and not know her...

VICTOR   Came a few days ago with the rest of the post, fully stamped.

MAURICE   A wife sending such a letter to her husband?

VICTOR   Posted from our own post office at the bottom of the road and written, presumably, in the lounge while I was here in the bedroom.

MAURICE   Just like that? For no reason?

VICTOR   Oh don't ask me about her. The children always used to tease her: 'Frustrated messenger from God!'

Graeme once described her. 'Yes,' Hilda would
say, 'overweight from under work!' She loved their
teasing.

They drink in silence.

*MAURICE knows his friend wants to talk about his
illness, and waits.*

*VICTOR dips his cake in the tea, sucks the juice from
it, bites, and begins.*

It began about three years ago. In the middle of
a strike. I began to suffer from headaches and
dizziness.

MAURICE   The hospital workers' strike?

VICTOR   Aye. Remember? Daft government policies.
What a time that was. All-night discussions about
compromise, open-air gatherings up and down the
country – the lot! So, blood pressure, I thought; and
went for a check-up. Nothing! Blood pressure was
high but not pathological. My general condition was
good. Next day, a phone call. Specialist's assistant.
Would I go in and see them. Something's cropped
up: When I saw the specialist next day – he told me:
high white corpuscle count. Just like that. Almost
angrily, as though I were to blame. Like being told
I'd got an overdraft.

And then, well, I was – curious. I was curious about
what I was going through. Curious, you know, like
a bystander. It were strange. I'd no sense of shock
or fear, no sweating or increased pulse. Just a great
slowing-down of time. Everything…in slow motion.
No, don't ask me to be logical about it. I only know
what happened. In this order, as I'm telling you.
And then, into this slow motion, came this great
increase of…don't laugh, it's difficult for me to say
it…but, this…great increase of love. I didn't feel it.
It wasn't that. But I had, suddenly, a better sense of
it. And then, relief. I was aware of how tired life had
made me, how tired I was of myself and how, now,

now I could be held responsible for nothing more:
Ever again. Sonia asked what it were and I told her
it were the strike. But she'd seen me in strike times
before, so I had to tell her half the truth, that I'd seen
a doctor and he'd told me to go easy because of high
blood pressure. Anyway, 'We're not certain,' the
specialist said, 'but all the evidence points to myeloid
leukaemia.' I knew the implication of that of course,
but I wanted to hear it spelt out. 'Fifty per cent of the
people in your condition live for ten years,' he said,
'of the other fifty per cent many live for five, some
for three. A few have been known to live for twenty
but that's rare. Some have died within the year but
that's just as rare. You have my answer.'

Ha! I had his answer all right. But, as you said; they
can be wrong. It's been known. So I saw someone
else. And what a bastard he turned out to be. A
diehard old Tory who'd obviously always hated my
guts. When I asked him for a prognosis he said: 'If
you've got some papers that need signing you can
leave them, but if you've got a fortune to make I'd
start making it right now.' I ignored all that and just
asked about the possibility of cure or spontaneous
recovery. And you know what he said? 'Cure is a
dirty word!' A right bastard he were. It was from
my own doctor, my own old GP that I managed to
find a little comfort. I remember he embraced me
first and then said: 'Vic, you aren't worried about
it are you? You're not going to die of leukaemia. A
heart attack, maybe, a plane crash; anything! But
not leukaemia. Myeloid leukaemia,' he said, 'for a
person in your condition and at your age is a benign
ailment. Eat very well. Go to bed early. Get up a bit
later. Avoid infections. Keep outdoors as much as
possible, and don't tell anybody, it only creates the
wrong atmosphere.' Great man, that. Restored my
sanity. So, there it is. I belonged to the fifty per cent
who last three years. My time's up. The Myleran and
Purinethol are having less and less effect. I'm up and

I'm down. I recover but I recover more slowly. It still just looks like high blood pressure to Sonia but I know. I know what's happening.

VICTOR is exhausted. MAURICE rises, anxious.

It's all right, just a turn.

MAURICE   You look so – so grey.

VICTOR   Grey is it? Ha! I'll be all right after a sleep. But you'd better go. Come again soon. Tomorrow, the day after. Leave the bloody students. Attend to me. I really need you, Maurice lad. But don't I beg you, don't tell Sonia.

SCENE 4

Lights up in garden area. Sound of brisk wind and crack of linen on a clothes-line.

SONIA (VO)   You used to tease me about God.

SONIA comes to hang up dazzling white sheets and pillow-slips.

Soft brain I had in them days. Could I help it though? My soft brain, yes, but not my religiousness. That were my upbringing. No one can be blamed for that, though they do say the sins of the fathers shall fall upon the sons; but that's cruel and unreasonable. Not that you were like that, you weren't cruel and unreasonable no, never, I'm not saying that. But you teased and you shouldn't have done because I was badly hurt by it. You didn't know that I was; but I was. Very hurt. To begin with. Then my brain got hard.

SONIA turns to go back for more linen but in turning finds she's facing the sun. She closes her eyes, basking in it, as the voice continues.

'God is one man's invention to frighten other men into being good,' you said. 'But no one's good if they're frightened.' That's what you said and it sounded very reasonable to me. Besides, there was the war and all of them soldiers being gassed and slaughtered and then it happened to my brother Stan so I couldn't much believe in God. But I missed him. I don't mind telling you I missed God. Used to give me lovely pictures to think about. It was a long time before I knew what it was you gave me. Better. You know that don't you?

> *Lights down in garden area. Up in VICTOR's room.*
>
> *Unbearably sad he cuddles one of the huge pillows for memory.*

After the teasing and tormenting my brain got harder and I grew proud of what I got to understand and how I could listen to you and your mates arguing and saving the world and make up my own mind. Did you know I grew? Couldn't talk or argue much or write but I grew. From God to you. Became a woman. For a while at least.

SCENE 5

VICTOR rises, moves to window.

MAURICE enters.

VICTOR Can't bear heavy skies. Sooner imagine it was night-time than face morbid bloody clouds. Look at those stunned starched overfed cushions. They reproduce themselves when I'm not looking. (*Beat.*) Well?

MAURICE (*Thinking he means SONIA's second letter.*) Extraordinary. Worth publishing.

VICTOR No! Not that daft thing. My notes I mean. The notes for my book.

MAURICE (*Returning folder.*) Ah, yes, well, those are also very well worth publishing.

VICTOR Aren't they a mess!

MAURICE All first drafts are a mess, Victor, not even erudite me gets it right first time.

VICTOR   A mess! Confused. Gibberish.

> *Complains but nevertheless makes holes with a*
> *hole-cutter to file his notes.*

When I wrote all that down I thought it was the
beginning of a profound inquiry that would unravel
why everyone concludes it's a rotten life.

> *Gives up trying to punch holes – his fingers can't bear*
> *pressure. Passes task to MAURICE.*

Have you noticed that? Everyone says it's a rotten
life, 'People are rotten!' Life; literature – all filled
with characters whose experience of the world is
depressing. So – who upsets them? Speak to the man
who they say has upset them and you find he also
thinks the world is a rotten place and that people are
rotten. And who's upset him? Where does it begin?
Everyone knows it's a terrible life only it never
seems possible to lay your finger on the culprit, the
cause. I know people have got answers – religious,
political, philosophic. But at the end of everyone's
life, whether he's a revolutionary leader, a dictator,
a pope, a millionaire – a worker, a prime minister,
a socialist citizen, a citizen of the West – a great
artist, a great scientist, a great philosopher – for all of
them! Terrible life! By the end of it they're all weary
and disillusioned and dispirited. I mean – listen to
Ruskin.

> *Reaches for a book.*

Who could want to have achieved more? But was he
happy?

(*Reads.*) 'I forget, now, what I meant by "liberty"
in this passage; but I often used the word in my
first writings in a good sense, thinking of Scott's
moorland rambles and the like. It is very wonderful
to me, now, to see what hopes I had once: but
Turner was alive then, and the sun used to shine, and
the rivers to sparkle.'

Too late, Maurice lad. Were a trade union leader too long. Should've given up at forty and started to study for me book then. But not now.

MAURICE Come on.

VICTOR Not even with your help.

Long pause. Suddenly:

Tell me about someone dying.

MAURICE About what?

VICTOR Someone dying. Someone you knew.

MAURICE Victor that's morbid.

VICTOR No it's not. It's sensible.

MAURICE We should be talking about your carefully filed-away gibberish.

VICTOR My carefully filed-away gibberish can take care of itself. Tell me.

MAURICE I can't. I'd be embarrassed.

VICTOR It's no use me ducking it. And besides, I want to talk about it.

MAURICE Don't make it more difficult for me than it is, for Christ's sake.

VICTOR I want to know. Familiarise myself with it. Tell me. Was there anyone? A friend? A relative? Someone close who you watched? A parent? There was your mother wasn't there? I remember that time. Tell me.

Long pause.

MAURICE She didn't know she was dying. Her kidneys… She was constipated and vomiting all the time. No appetite… Victor, I can't.

VICTOR Please.

MAURICE It was her bewilderment distressed me most. She was living with us by this time, and as the days went by she'd eat a little, complain of pain in her gums, vomit while I held her head, and then say,

'When? When, when will it be over, done, finished
with?' She couldn't understand. 'I've never been
so ill. Never!' She'd be angry but she'd make jokes.
On her good days, when she could eat and not feel
nauseous, she'd sit up, hold out her hand and cross
her fingers. 'Don't say anything,' she'd caution, 'just
hope!' And when I'd given her her umpteen pills
she'd say, 'Well, I'm a good pill-taker at least.' Once
when the doctor came and she was particularly
flat-out, collapsed utterly into her pillows, he asked
in that special breezy voice doctors reserve for
the dying, 'And how are you today?' She replied
with her special brand of gentle self-mockery, and
holding her aching gums: 'Oh, very well, thank you.'
I remember once when I was sitting by her she held
a little hand mirror in front of her and after looking
for a while she said: 'How? How could I become
such a face, how?' and she clutched at the side of
her head and rocked it as though trying to shake her
mind and memory back into place.

Then she stopped, and said simply, 'I want no fuss,
you know what I mean? No fuss. It's got to come
sometime or other, sooner or later.' I pretended she
was talking nonsense. Got angry with her, even. But
she persisted. 'I might go any time. Suddenly. Plonk!
Finished! What can you do?' I didn't think I'd ever
weep, but I did. It was an absurd time. Weeping.
Everything about her and everything associated
with her became very vivid and unbearably dear to
me. As though my unhappiness gave each detail of
memory an extra meaning. I had to keep driving
to her flat to look for mail, reassure the neighbours,
collect her pension, and even driving up to the
council estate, even just the act of swerving the
car into the curb, an action I'd done a hundred
times before, caused me to swallow hard because
I associated it with driving to see her and finding
her writing her diary, watching television, cooking
or just standing in front of the gas stove hoping the

warmth from the upper grill would ease the pain
in her gums. Memory of her flooded back at every
corner. I was covering ground I knew she'd never
cover again. It was all poignant, full of loneliness,
that quadrangle of other old people, looking out of
windows, waiting. Full of loneliness and a sense of
time past. Sad. I can remember an overwhelming
ache to be young again with her, cooking for my
friends, telling me off for late hours but joining in.
And she'd make it worse by trying to make it seem
the most natural thing in the world. Which it is.
Only it never seems so. 'I don't mind,' she'd say.
'Only peace, let there be peace in the world, and
friendship in the family. Stay together. Don't be sad.
I don't really mind.'

MAURICE sits on the bed beside VICTOR.

As she became worse the pain in her gums increased
and she needed to be kept on Palfium drugs.
Morphine based. She'd get high, lose her memory,
construct strange or unfinished sentences. 'I'll soon
tell you, I'll soon tell you all about it.' About what?
God knows! She never finished. Once I went into
her room and found her sitting up and clutching at
something in the air, as though reaching out for a
person, and she said, 'Suddenly, just then, I felt that
really I was alone.' In the end not all the pills I gave
her helped, so I sat close to her and cradled her in
my arms instead, holding her hands. 'Ah, warmth,
warmth!' she said, 'there's nothing like warmth.' (*He
cradles VICTOR.*) 'Get into bed,' I said, 'that'll make
you warm.' 'Not warm like this,' she said.

Pause.

A few days before she died I went into her room
– I'd go there first thing as soon as I got up – she
was sitting with her hands behind her head, her eyes
bright. 'I feel so excited about something', she said.
'I want something to happen, some event, some
special event.' I took her downstairs, walking in front

of her, holding her hand, high up, to steady her. She descended, slowly, sedately. 'The bride!' she said.

Pause.

And all the time the vomiting, the pain in the gums, the jokes and the bewilderment.

Pause.

Jokes and the bewilderment.

Pause.

Jokes.

Pause.

She was a tiny thing. So sweet.

Pause.

I adored her.

They exchange smiles. It is a moment of gentle rapport.

SCENE 6

Sound of telephone. It's picked up. Sound of MAURICE'S VOICEOVER.

Lights up on lounge. VICTOR on phone.

MAURICE (VO) Victor?

VICTOR Aye, it's me.

MAURICE (VO) I'm sorry, Vic, but I won't be able to come when I promised. I have to go to the States.

VICTOR (*Sourly.*) Are you trying to pretend that'll be an unpleasant labour for you?

MAURICE (VO) Don't be angry with me, friend. It's only two weeks. A colleague's gone down with a sudden appendix and I've got to take over his lecture tour.

VICTOR I'm sure you'll have a terrible time.

MAURICE (VO) Of course I won't have a terrible time. Don't begrudge it to me. I've not been abroad these last

five years: But I'll come and see you as soon as I
return. Even jet-lagged.

VICTOR (*Whispering.*) I've had another of those letters.

MAURICE (VO) From Sonia?

VICTOR Aye. A third one. I'll send it you. Read it on the
plane. Ssh. No more, she's coming. Safe journey.

Puts down phone.

SCENE 7

*The kitchen where SONIA is laying out two cups and saucers
on a tray already laid up with a pot of tea and jug of milk.*

SONIA (VO) The only time I ever swore was a night you got more
than normal drunk and wept because things weren't
going right in the union and you began complaining
at me. You told me, 'You don't care about me or my
state or the fact that I'm losing me nerve and failing
me mates, do you? And you haven't a care for rights
nor conditions nor wages nor nothing.' Remember
that?

*From oven she pulls a platter of scones, prises off
two, slices them in half, takes from fridge a bowl of
double-whipped cream, spreads it over the four halves
of scone, returns bowl, then without bending her legs,
stoops to a cupboard for strawberry jam which she
drips over cream, during which –*

How you raged and wept and screamed. 'I'm going
to pieces, I'm going to pieces and you don't care
and you don't understand.' Very loud you were that
night my love, and I railed back, 'Of course I care
of course I understand but I won't give consolations
to a man when he's filled with pity and shit. That's
what you are,' I said, 'you're filled with pity and
shit.' Ha! The only time you wept and I swore that
was.

*SONIA smiles to herself. The change from her normal
severity is stunning.*

Bright sunlight floods the garden area and spreads into the bedroom.

VICTOR is putting on his dressing-gown. Wraps a scarf around his neck, moves into the garden.

SONIA takes linen off clothes-line and, though silent, yet she is happily defiant.

And that was a tense time. Very tense that was, my love. I'm laughing as I write it down. You looked so funny, so startled. I felt very bucked with myself to have startled you so. It was serious then but I confess how I giggled afterwards. Went away and giggled to myself I'm laughing even as I write about it. Oh dear. Ha ha!' Full of pity and shit!' I said. You forgot all about your going to pieces then. Aye. You were so shocked. Pity and shit! Ha! Ha!

SONIA brings tray to a garden table, facing the sun. She removes scarf from her neck, and places it round VICTOR's. Feigns strangling him, a tender, playful moment.

SCENE 8

MAURICE arrives, helps to bring chairs to the table.

SONIA leaves. The friends embrace.

VICTOR   And how was the land of the bitch goddess?

MAURICE   I can't make up my mind about the American success bitch. Like many bitches, in the process of chewing you up she brings every nerve-end alive. (*Pause.*) How are you?

VICTOR   Would you believe it, she wants me to get out of bed, pack a case and go with her for a week to Mytholmroyd on the moors, where we used to court. Isn't that daft? Now that's a daft thing for you. Doesn't she know I'm bloody dy– No! She doesn't, poor bitch! It's no good, Maurice, I can't take it. I thought I had it in me but I haven't. I'm so frightened and unhappy. You think something

will happen, someone – a discovery in time.
Something always did, didn't it? Whenever we made
fools of ourselves or got ill there was help, a cure,
forgiveness. I can't really be dying! That's just plain
silly. What? All this – gone, stopped, done? It's such
a burden this knowledge, rotten, heavy. I feel so
humiliated watching myself become frightened. No
one should have to know it. It's not fair. A man's
not made to live with such a knowledge. Look at it!
(*Waves arm at sky and garden.*) Love it! I love it, love
it! I just plain and simply love it! (*He weeps.*) Bloody
hell! Don't let her see me like this. There'll be
murder to pay. Kill me, she would.

> *This amuses him. He smiles. Smile grows into laughter, into exhaustion.*

> *MAURICE retrieves a mounted drawing from his briefcase.*

MAURICE Here! Found it in a little junk shop in New Bedford.
Look at it carefully. What's the signature?

> *VICTOR reaches for some glasses.*

VICTOR (*Peering.*) John Rushton? Who's John Rushton?

MAURICE Are you sure it says Rushton? That's what I thought,
but look again.

VICTOR (*Testily.*) Rushton. It says Rushton. That's all I can
see. (*Returns drawing.*)

MAURICE (*Whispering.*) What about – Ruskin?

> *VICTOR is suddenly alert and snatches back the drawing.*

VICTOR Ruskin?

> *Takes a huge magnifying glass from dressing-gown pocket. Squints. Excitedly.*

My God, it could be. It just could be. Now isn't
that a thrill! Well, that's revived me no end that
has. You're a lovely friend. Was worth pushing you
through college. Forgive me jadedness, I mean – a
Ruskin! Well!

Pause.

There's no doubt about it, the soul *does* depend upon the body.

Refills his cup, clasps it, walks to bottom of garden. A cricket field in view.

He watches the slow mechanics of the game.

Sound of birds and the knock of ball on wood.

I've started to imagine this other place.

MAURICE 'Avoid infections. Keep outdoors as much as possible...'

VICTOR Supposing it did exist.

MAURICE '...and don't tell anybody,' your doctor said.

VICTOR But just supposing.

MAURICE 'It only creates the wrong atmosphere,' he said.

VICTOR What could it be like? I mean I can't even begin to imagine what it would be like visually. Where do you place it, this...afterlife? And then I think: it's not a physical place, Victor, that's where you go wrong: It's a spiritual state, a state of awareness unconfined by a physical framework. Ha! And so I lie in there trying to project myself into 'a spiritual state of awareness unconfined by a physical framework'! Ever tried to do that?

MAURICE Often!

VICTOR Try it some day. And then I get angry and I say to myself: 'Darkness! Nothing! When you're dead that's it. Over! Done! If you want satisfaction, Victor lad, then look to your life, your political battles, the fights you fought for other men.' But who can do that for long? Dwell on his past and go scratching for bits of victory? Eh? A smug man perhaps. But I'm not a smug man, Maurice, never was. So what's left? No afterlife I can conceive of and no past to feel at peace with. And I go round and round in circles driving myself mad because even the very

act of contemplating it, me! Thinking about whether
there's a heaven, another life, the very worrying
about such things makes me feel guilty and shabby.
'You, Victor? Worrying about where you're going?
Frightened are you?' I taunt myself: 'Frightened?
Poor, feeble-minded man, you. You who used to be
so confident about it all beginning with birth and
ending with death. You! Want a comfortable little
heaven to go to now? Do you? And I'm a merciless
bugger you know. Really get to the heart of myself,
where it hurts. Always been like that. Have you ever
thought about the tone of voice your conscience has?
Everyone's got a conscience which talks to them in a
different tone of voice. Mine jeers. Very acidy. (*Picks
up drawing.*) A Ruskin. What d'you know?

SONIA   (*Calling.*) Victor! You haven't forgotten?

VICTOR   Noa, noa, lass! You wouldn't believe it but when
there's no one in the house she's a changed woman.
Becomes visibly younger, playful and tender. You
know how it is when some people are angry, they
turn, well, ugly. Their face collapses. Get defeated
by their own irritation, become heavy, vicious. She
even treats *me* like a stranger then. But when they
leave she's full of outrage and she's magnificent.
I love her! Even that massive bulk of hers moves
elegantly. Now she's heavy as a landslide because
a gaggle of old colleagues are due in half an hour
– God knows what for.

MAURICE   Is that my cue to go?

VICTOR   Good God, no! Just wait out here while I change. I'm
not letting that lot see me in bedclothes.

> *VICTOR returns to bedroom.*
>
> *MAURICE sits back, closes eyes, takes in the sun.*
>
> *SONIA collects cups and saucers in stern silence.*
>
> *As she leaves –*

MAURICE   (*Exploding.*) Sonia, stop this. For Christ's sake. It's
not an easy world and I'm far from being the most

perfect of men but you've been given no cause to be
so unfriendly. Even if only because your husband
needs our friendship you ought to show more grace.

*SONIA is untouched. As she returns to the kitchen
MAURICE grabs a scone from the tray getting his
fingers sticky.*

*Re-enters the lounge irritated. But it's a comical
moment.*

*Meanwhile VICTOR calls SONIA to look at his
drawing. She peers at the signature through the
magnifying glass.*

SONIA   Rushton?

VICTOR   What about Ruskin?

SONIA   Ruskin? John Ruskin? (*Peers again. Is pleased for him.*)
          Aren't you the lucky one!

*MAURICE looks around the room. Nonchalantly picks
up a beautiful cut-glass wineglass, holds it up to the
sunlight, twirls it round, reflects it on the palm of his
hand. The pleasure of it dims his irritability.*

*He sits by the desk, swivels round and round until
he catches sight of familiar sheets of blue paper
stuck in between the pages of a huge Oxford English
Dictionary.*

*Hesitantly, guiltily, he opens the book, lifts out the
sheets, and begins to read aloud.*

MAURICE   'The lilac is dead: Don't ask me how but it's had a
          blight. Remember the lilac? We planted it forty-one
          years ago and uprooted it four times for four changes
          of house.

SONIA's voice merges into MAURICE's.

It survived all those up-rootings and now…

SONIA (VO) I'd be lost without my garden.

*SONIA, armed with secateurs and garden gloves enters
garden to cut eight roses for a vase.*

Returns to kitchen, fills vase with water, snips excess foliage, arranges them.

During all that we hear letter.

Sunlight floods the kitchen.

It's not just a place I potter around in you know. I think you think it is. 'Thank God she's occupied,' you say to yourself I bet. No, it's a place where I think my best thoughts, my only thoughts in fact even though they don't amount to many. And where I touch all manner of things like earth and leaves, squashed worms and stones and colours and fresh air and smells and winds and clouds and rain and sunlight and – the cycle of things. You used to be like that, loving the cycle of things. It's you I got it from. Remember how the lilac came? You brought it home one day and said we must start a garden. You'd got it from the old railway porter. It was a sucker and you told me, lilac cuttings were always suckers; from the roots not the branch. A thin thing it was with only a few whispery strands between living and dying. I didn't think it would take but you did and it started our garden off.

She looks at her watch. The trade unionists will soon be here.

On a highly polished copper tray she places five cut-glass sherry glasses and a bottle of sherry, which she pours out into an exquisite cut-glass decanter.

From this she meticulously measures out five just adequate drinks. In one she has put too much and sips the excess herself, which she likes, so she finishes it and has to measure another.

With the same care she spreads ten sponge fingers around a willow pattern plate.

Pours herself another glass of sherry, sits and waits.

The letter has continued meanwhile.

What about those arguments we had? We had our fast rows over our first garden. What shape it should be, what should grow in it, which way it should face. You would insist the sun came up in one place while I knew darn well it came up in another. So what did we do? Daft buggers – we set the alarm to get up before sunrise. You were wrong of course. You've no idea how important it was to me to have been right about that. It was my first landmark. Gave me great confidence that did.

> *VICTOR is looking through his wardrobe to decide which outfit to wear. Resignedly realises he doesn't really care and settles for a light brown check suit with waistcoat.*
>
> *He takes off his dressing-gown, his pyjama top, puts on a shirt, his trousers, a tie, slowly, slowly…through all of which we've heard –*

And as for the quarrels about what we should grow, well – I thought it would end our marriage. I wanted more veggies and you wanted more flowers. You said it wasn't a real saving to grow our own veggies, only an illusion. But you said, all right, we'll have more veggies only I had to keep accounts. You made me work out what it cost in seed and labour and I had to weigh all what grew and then check it with the price in markets and make a sum of it all. And I did it too. Worked all hours figuring it out. Mad people. But I loved it. Columns of figures all very neat, and grand headings. Looked very important. I got top marks at school for neatness. Loved it. And was I proud. I was proud. Gave me great pleasure and I was right. Again. It did pay to grow our own veggies. That was my second landmark. A huge garden. Planted everything in it bar the sun.

When you insisted I learn to drive a car, that was a landmark. When you asked me to show the Italian delegation round London without you, that was a landmark. When you first went abroad for a fortnight and I carried my affairs and your affairs alone without you, that was a landmark. When you first put your head between my legs, that was a landmark...when...

> *Lights up sharply upon an embarrassed MAURICE who hurriedly pushes the sheets into the dictionary.*

SCENE 9

At that same moment the house moves into action.

A doorbell rings. SONIA moves to lounge with sherry and flowers.

VICTOR, dressed, braces himself and also moves to lounge.

Both SONIA and MAURICE register with shock how thin VICTOR looks in the clothes he's not worn for so long.

SONIA moves to go to front door, but is stopped by VICTOR.

VICTOR Don't rush. They can wait. One before they come?

> *He drinks a sherry.*
>
> *VICTOR has observed nothing, but the moment has brought together MAURICE and SONIA.*
>
> *Front doorbell rings again.*
>
> *SONIA moves to answer door.*
>
> *Blackout.*
>
> *Babble of conversation carried over until lights up on lounge, bedroom and kitchen.*
>
> *VICTOR exhausted in lounge armchair.*
>
> *MAURICE tray in hand in the kitchen with SONIA.*

SONIA (*Taking tray.*) He looked so thin.

MAURICE It went well.

SONIA Those clothes, they hang so – so pointlessly on him.

MAURICE They came to ask if they could name a new trade union building in his name.

SONIA So – alien on him.

MAURICE   (*Imitating.*) 'I'm fundamentally opposed to a building being named after anyone – ' (*Beat.*) – 'but I'd love to see myself made an exception of.' His performance was a joy.

SONIA   Oh aye! He could always perform for them.

MAURICE   'On one condition,' he said, 'that you assure and promise me a sum of money will be set aside for purchasing the paintings and prints of young artists to go on the walls. You've known it's been my passion to help young painters and civilise you barbarians.'

SONIA   Aye! Used to squeeze between their prejudices and bloody-mindedness like a political Geiger counter. The rank and file loved him for it. Not the hierarchy, though. All they did was tire him out. Couldn't trust him. What! Trust a man without political ambitions?

> *She moves to lounge.*
>
> *VICTOR is raising himself with difficulty, she moves swiftly to help him.*

That's what they did, always. Drained you!

> *He kisses her hand as she helps him up.*
>
> *She withdraws it, speaking with kindly severity as she guides him towards the bedroom.*
>
> *He mumbles affectionately, teasingly.*

Selfish men! You only ever surrounded yourself with selfish men who used you, built their careers on you and then left you. A once-and-only lifetime, wasted on them. Selfish men! (*Calling after them.*) SELFISH MEN!

> *VICTOR turns to MAURICE who stands with briefcase in hand.*

VICTOR   You're not going, are you?

MAURICE   I think you need to rest, dear friend.

VICTOR   Wait. Help me undress and then you can go. Ten minutes. What's ten minutes to you?

MAURICE appeals to SONIA with another look. She nods. Leaves, but kisses and, for the first time, smiles at him.

MAURICE My first kiss from Sonia in months!

He helps VICTOR undress.

VICTOR She's always been like that. Anxious about abuse. Me, I never worry. Hell! It were a lonely life. In order to find one friend you had to let dozens abuse you, I reckoned. I always took it easy. Not her, though, she scowled. Let the lads come I always said, they ate a little, drank, lingered. My family's atmosphere was like that – open house. Not her, though. Give everything to the friends she loved, but everything. Mean as old socks to the rest.

SCENE 10

The kitchen. SONIA is spreading out a newspaper on the table ready to polish brass. Puts on rubber gloves. Furiously and angrily polishes.

MAURICE patiently waits, watching SONIA, and reading newspaper.

A visitor is with VICTOR, a young trade union OFFICIAL. Business talks are more or less over and he's looking at paintings.

VICTOR And one last thing – before you go – while you're on strike losing your week's wages, which you can ill afford, while you're being loyal and comradely and losing your wages do you know where your General Secretary is?

OFFICIAL No, where?

VICTOR In the bloody Canary Islands having a bloody holiday.

OFFICIAL Bloody Canary Islands?

VICTOR Yes, R S bloody D, your General bloody Secretary, having a bloody holiday and looking for a house to

buy for himself out of union bloody funds for when
he retires.

OFFICIAL Bloody Canary Islands! Now isn't that just like R S
bloody D. (*Referring to painting.*) Nice.

VICTOR (*Taking painting from him.*) You're not appalled?

OFFICIAL It's not a perfect world is it.

VICTOR He's not appalled.

OFFICIAL Aren't we being a little naive, Victor?

VICTOR I think you'd better be off. I get tired.

OFFICIAL Look Vic. We all know how it goes on and some of
us aren't happy about it. But let's stick to the agenda,
first things first. This wildcat strike. Trust me! The
lads'll be interested in what I tell them you've said,
you'll see, your advice is going to make great sense.

VICTOR And I'd be obliged if you didn't misinterpret me.

OFFICIAL Not me. They'll appreciate every word.

VICTOR But not take any notice.

OFFICIAL Ah, well. The offer of advice and the taking of notice
are two different things, as we all know.

VICTOR As we do indeed all know.

OFFICIAL But the lads will listen.

VICTOR You promise me that?

OFFICIAL Why shouldn't they? They're good lads. Bit
opinionated, without thought sometimes, but you're
something of a legend for them.

VICTOR Unbelievable you mean!

OFFICIAL They'll respect every word you said. I didn't tell
them I was coming to see you, but it came to me,
suddenly – ask Victor, he'll know the arguments to
use for pointless strikes. I'm like that: impulsive. An
idea strikes me? I'm away. Vroom! First from the pit.
Vroom! Can't sleep at nights for the ideas that dance
in me. Ask Victor – Vroom! Vic always knows.

VICTOR   Not always. Wish I did. Wish ideas danced in me. Vroom! Might've done more with me life, but...

OFFICIAL   More? Few people in the movement achieved more than you, Vic.

VICTOR   Yes, yes.

OFFICIAL   No, no! Don't sell yourself short. You're a yardstick for us youngsters.

VICTOR   Please, I really do get tired.

OFFICIAL   Yes, of course, I do go on. But I want you to know, Vic, I'm your man in the office. Anything I can do –

VICTOR   Vroom!

OFFICIAL   Anything you want –

VICTOR   Thank you, thank you.

OFFICIAL   Ask me.

VICTOR   Yes.

OFFICIAL   I'm your man.

VICTOR   Goodbye then.

OFFICIAL   And I won't misinterpret you.

VICTOR   Of course not. Goodbye.

OFFICIAL   Someone else might've come. Taken your advice, twisted it to his own ends and given it the authority of your blessing.

VICTOR   Oh?

OFFICIAL   Not me, though.

VICTOR   Good.

OFFICIAL   I am the best person. The doctor did say blood pressure?

VICTOR   Aye, blood pressure.

OFFICIAL   I mean, we've got our own hospital, Vic. A great team of specialists, to...

VICTOR   I know. I did help found it!

OFFICIAL   Of course. Goodbye then. Are you sure…? Keep
           well now. If you… Don't do anything rash.

> *VICTOR thankfully grabs the hand offered him.*
>
> *The OFFICIAL has to leave. On his way out…*

The paintings read well.

> *Pauses, turns.*

Vroom!

> *Calls to SONIA.*

Goodbye then, Mrs M.

SONIA   Oh, he knew he had to go, then!

> *The OFFICIAL waits for her to see him out.*
>
> *She doesn't move.*

OFFICIAL   No, don't bother. I'll see myself out. He's looking
           very well, so don't you worry. Anything we can do
           don't you forget to contact us and we'll…

SONIA   Don't forget to close the door firmly when you go
        out.

> *Gives up. Leaves.*
>
> *MAURICE prepares lemon barley water for VICTOR.*

Patronising little upstarts! Nothing can touch them.
Watch him go back and say to his bumptious little
colleagues, 'Well I had a word with old Vic and he
agreed with me this and he agreed with me that!'
Bloody little opportunist! Unioncrats I call them.
Rattie-catties. That's it, Maurice, take him his drink,
he'll be needing it after that demoralising encounter.
Here.

> *Reaches for brandy to lace drink.*
>
> *SONIA slides to her place behind desk in lounge.*
>
> *MAURICE takes tray to bedroom.*

SCENE 11

VICTOR is scrutinising his drawing through a huge magnifying glass.

VICTOR   My bloody eyesight's going. They told me that
          would go. Jesus Christ I just have to sit here and
          watch myself disintegrate. But you know, Maurice,
          I think it is a Ruskin. Look, compare it with this
          facsimile of his signature. It's shakier than the other,
          that's all. Mine's an early sketch, but… Now how in
          hell did it get to New Bedford I wonder? *There's* a
          story for someone. What lives were wrapped around
          the voyage of that, eh?

MAURICE   Who was the badly dressed, smart young man?

VICTOR   A young 'father' from one of the printing chapels.
          They want to come out on a token sympathy strike
          with the footplate men.

          Smells drink.

          Whose birthday, luv? You know what the real
          problem is with industrial relations? To sort out
          the true militants from the holidaymakers. There's
          a lot of them. And they're bullies with it. Cheap
          Chicago-style mobsters. When I told that fellow
          his union boss was buying himself a house in the
          Canary Islands out of union finds you know what
          he did? You won't believe it – he nudged me and he
          said, 'Now isn't that just like R S D'. *Admired* it! He
          admired his union boss being like all the employers
          so's to show they could screw their way into power
          and affluence same as them. Doesn't that depress
          you? Depresses the hell out of me. Can't win now,
          Maurice. Capitalism has created an enemy in its own
          image, monstrous as itself. Hurts. What a mess, eh?
          What a waste. What a life. Would you get the Ruskin
          framed for me, please?

MAURICE   Surely.

VICTOR   For Sonia.

Both men realise they're looking at the made-up bed with its dazzling white sheets and high-stacked white pillows.

I mean, sometimes I feel guilty for dozing on them of an afternoon I fear she might come up and change them twice a day.

VICTOR wraps blanket round his shoulders, for comfort, preparing to say something special.

MAURICE waits.

They want me in hospital. A few days, week maybe, for preliminary tests, you know the sort of thing. Think they may have found a new drug.

MAURICE   Found a new drug! What good news! Why look so down? Don't you know what scientists can do these days?

VICTOR   You think so? Well, I could more easily bring myself to believe in the possibility of a cure than an afterlife.

MAURICE   You still dwelling on such morbid prospects?

VICTOR   Even if I'm cured, Maurice lad, it won't ever stop me thinking about the afterlife. Been too near to leave off contemplating it now. Here.

Gives MAURICE one letter on blue paper and holds on to another.

Two arrived in one day. How about that?

MAURICE reads.

SCENE 12

Lights up in lounge from where SONIA reads.

A duet ensues between husband and wife.

SONIA   On the day we got married I thought you hated me. I must tell you that, because it's the only time I've ever seen hate in your eyes.

VICTOR   She wrote one, sealed the envelope, wrote another and didn't open the first to put them together, no! Posted them separately! Do you think there's something wrong in her blood also?

SONIA What am I doing marrying a man who hates me, I thought to myself? You were so silent, so angry. But afterwards – well – I didn't ever say but I used never to be able to take my eyes off you.

VICTOR (*Complaining.*) When can I remember?

SONIA No one had ever been so tender and certain.

VICTOR I can't remember things.

SONIA And you used to sing.

VICTOR She used to laugh a lot.

SONIA Once a visitor came from abroad –

VICTOR In the early days.

SONIA I can't remember where, France...I think...and he said to me, 'Good God, there's someone who can still sing.'

VICTOR In the early days she used to laugh a great deal. At predicaments!

SONIA Our first son sang also.

VICTOR When an innocent bystander was caught up in someone else's confusion – that! That amused her.

SONIA I remember we'd wake and find him standing up in his cot looking down on us, not crying, not murmuring, nor nothing, just patiently waiting for us to wake up. And when we did he was the first thing we looked at and he knew it and waited for it and then gave us a slow smile and started to hum. Nearly every morning was like that.

VICTOR Once, when she was learning to drive, she came out of a side-turning too quickly, and another car, coming across our path and with the right of way to pass straight in front of us, was forced to turn right into the street opposite us, which he did and went straight on. God knows why he didn't stop and tell her off. And she laughed! She laughed till she ached.

'He didn't want to go down that street,' she kept
saying. 'Poor man! He was on his way to one place
and now he's got to go somewhere else!'

SONIA   You were daft about our son.

VICTOR   That did amuse her that did. Laughed till tears came.
And she looked beautiful with it.

SONIA   Wanted him to be a composer.

VICTOR   I remember. Radiant.

SONIA   You used to play classical records in the bedroom
while he was asleep. 'It's best it sinks into him
unconsciously,' you said. Weird theories you had.
You wouldn't ever tell him to think of music as a
career, that would put him off, but if it went in…if it
went in…

*SONIA leaves off writing and reaches for the Shorter
Oxford Dictionary.*

…now what was that word he used? Began with
an S. (*Flicks pages.*) P, Q, R, S. S! 'S' what? 'S' 'i'?
'Siderite – a steel coloured stone.' Well it wasn't that.
'Sibilate – to hiss.' It wasn't that either. What a lot
of lovely words. 'Solatium – a sum of money paid
for injured feelings.' 'Solazzi – a stick of liquorice.'
Liquorice? I always thought the word was lickerish.
I'm sure it was. (*Looking back to the 'L's.*) 'Lichen,
lichgate, licit, lick, lickpenny', ah! 'Lickerish'! 'To be
good like a cook at preparing dainties, stopped using
in 1600, used "likerous" instead.' Did they, now!
And what else have I been missing all these years I
wonder? Huh! (*Flicks back to 'S's.*) Ah ha! Subliminal!
That was it! Subliminally! (*Turns back to letter.*) That
would put him off, but if it went in subliminally…

Continues writing in silence, tongue out.

SONIA (VO)   There! See what writing to you does for me?

Puts sheets between pages of dictionary.

Moves to kitchen, continues polishing brass.

Where was I? Music! There was one day, my God
don't I remember that day, the children must've
been about nine and eleven and you took us up a
climb on the Peaks. Dangerous old route you took
us. You were scared too. You won't remember it but
you got us on to a tricky part where you had to go
back and forwards across a gap four times in order
to help me and the children, and you were sweating.
The children thought it was great fun. They would.
You would never let them be frightened of anything.
Not always a good thing I thought. Still, I remember
that trip for three reasons. The dangerous climb was
one. The other was you letting out by accident that
you'd had a girlfriend before me who'd climbed
with you on that same walk. You blushed when you
realised it'd been let out. In fact I wasn't sure if you
were talking about a girlfriend before me or after
me... And the third thing was the song we sang at
the top when we got there.

Voices singing – the family, adults and children,
forming a background to...

We ate sandwiches and there was a big wind and
you cried out like a madman, 'We must sing against
the wind. Good for the lungs and the spirit.' So you
taught us a round. The words were:
'By the waters, the waters of Babylon
We lay down and wept and wept
For these I am.
Thee remember thee remember thee remember
These I am.'

SONIA carries brass objects – candlesticks, trays,
ashtrays, horse brasses, etc – to lounge where a shaft
of light catches her thoughtfully and lovingly laying
them out.

What did it mean? I never knew what it meant. Not
all this time. 'We wept for these I am.' What are
'these I am'? Do you think you got it wrong? We all
used to get songs wrong as children. I used to think

it was 'Good King Wences last looked out', instead of 'Good King Wenceslas looked out'. Perhaps it should have been 'thee Zion'. Perhaps, we should have wept 'for thee Zion'. Or no –

Catches sight of her reflection in a brass tray, holds it up, her face is lit up but sad.

– no, now I come to think of it, you were probably right after all and we wept because I am these things, we are these things, all are these things.

Singing finishes.

SCENE 13

The bedroom.

VICTOR I could only remember the hair-raising climb. Nothing else.

MAURICE They're getting better. Each one more fluent than the last. It's obviously giving her great pleasure to write them.

VICTOR More fluent and madder. In this one she wants us to go on holiday to visit the children.

MAURICE So?

VICTOR So? So? All the way up to the Orkneys to see Graeme doing research on God-knows-what? Thank you! Here, help me make the bed, please.

Both men, having been in the forces, do it expertly, stripping it and remaking it with corner folds.

And we don't even know where Hilda and her husband are, some archaeological dig somewhere. (*Reading from letter.*) 'What's the good of all those savings to us when we're too old to use it that's what I say and you should say it too.' She's mad! We've got no savings. A few hundred pounds! Travel! Ha!

MAURICE She's not simply talking about travel, she's talking about plans to do things and it seems to me that on this hope of a new drug…

VICTOR (*Anger, despair.*) What new drug? It's not been tried yet. It might be 'that old drug'. And what plans? I've got plans. I want to write this book. What should I want to travel for? Haven't I done enough of that sort of thing? I'm tired now. Stupid woman!

She hated me being a trade union leader you know. Hated it. Man as a political or social animal she could never understand. People were good or bad, selfish or generous, sensible or idiots, never victims. Discussion, debate, the consideration of political principles – a foreign language! And it used to make her so angry that I was tied up in it all, she deliberately crept into the background. The years from forty to fifty were the worst. Like strangers we were. Hardly spoke. Terrible time, that. At least for us. But not funny, this – not for her. She seemed to grow. In confidence, cockiness, independence – some bloody thing or other. Grow, mature, take over. Aye, that was it, she took over, all but me General Secretaryship, became another woman, formidable, a huge presence.

Here, a few more notes for that bloody book. They're no good and it's a waste of everybody's time but could you keep the illusion going for me and have them typed, please?

MAURICE flicks through notes.

MAURICE Escher? The Dutch Artist? You're poking about in the obscure corners of the art world. Taken a liking to him?

VICTOR (*Wearily.*) No, I haven't taken a liking to him, and he's no longer an obscure artist. In fact there's quite a cult growing up around him. Unhealthy it seems to me. Read it. Or don't read it. Whatever you like.

MAURICE (*Reading.*) 'Escher delights in the cheatability of perspective.' 'Cheatability'?

VICTOR (*Mischievously grinning.*) Why not?

MAURICE   (*Continues reading.*) 'He seems unmoved by what
           moves man to contort his body or arrange the
           bones in his face. There's no face weeping, no eyes
           laughing, no body leaping, no figure suffering. Only
           the sterile, geometric shapes of life seem to obsess
           him, not life itself.' (*Pause.*) You're a very remarkable
           man, Victor, Ruskin would have been proud of you.
           Wasted on union matters.

VICTOR   Wasted? You think so? You're charitable. But the
           men had to be protected. You should have seen
           some of the employers I had to protect them from.
           Wished they hadn't needed protection, looked after
           their own bloody selves. But there it is. Done now.

           Sound of Janáček Sinfonietta.

MAURICE   What's that?

VICTOR   My mad wife. Whenever she hears a bit of music she
           likes she turns it up loudly so's I can hear it also.

           They listen a moment.

           *The passage is near the end of the Sinfonietta, the most
           vibrant part, full of tall mountains and echoes.*

MAURICE   Janáček.

VICTOR   Who?

MAURICE   Czech composer.

VICTOR   Oh.

           MAURICE prepares to leave.

           Don't neglect me, Maurice, don't forget your old
           friend.

           *MAURICE reassuringly squeezes his friend's shoulder,
           and leaves.*

           *He pauses at a point between a rapt SONIA listening
           to the music, and a dejected VICTOR, slouched, utterly
           miserable.*

MAURICE   (*Closing his eyes.*) It's not me, not me! Thank God it's
           not me, thank God it's not me.

Ashamed and depressed he covers his face with his hands.

Music rises to a crescendo as a hospital bed slides, like a crematorium box, into view.

VICTOR moves from one bed to the other as though to meet death.

Lights and music fade.

SCENE 14

Hospital bed. No white cushions starched crisp with love and protection. A metallic thing, of cleanliness only.

VICTOR sitting up in bed. MAURICE standing by, opening a briefcase.

VICTOR   It's going to be a long bloody job. Longer'n I thought. Longer'n they told me, in fact.

MAURICE   (*Handing him a folder.*) Your notes, typed.

VICTOR   (*Sitting up to look at them.*) Oh, aye. (*Reaches for his glasses. No use. Reaches for enormous magnifying glass.*) No good. It's no good. I'm going blind. Oh bloody Christ, Maurice!

MAURICE   They're good notes, Victor. Fine. Some things I don't agree with, you'd expect that, but it has the makings of a unique little book on art, I promise you.

   Pause.

VICTOR   You don't believe in God, do you, professor?

MAURICE   I don't really think I can.

VICTOR   Right! You can't. Nor can't I. But the ceasing for ever of all this – (*Knocks angrily on his skull.*) …that doesn't make sense either. Of course there are some people to whom it makes ecstatic sense, but they're a type, the put-downers I call them. Any bloody opportunity they get, they enjoy putting people down. They have a special tone of voice, the kind of voice that rubs its hands together. 'Look at the ocean,' they cry, 'see

what a little thing is man in all that sea!' And when
space-rockets came they had a real ball. 'Look at all
those stars. How insignificant is man now!' Instead
of marvelling that man could make it to the bloody
moon they found it another opportunity to put him
down. And now there's those stupid computers. Oh
how they do love putting people down because they
can't store up facts mechanically. But a computer's
a poor thing compared to a brain isn't it? I mean,
bloody hell! I'm no scientist but even I know that.
Can't store a shred of what the brain can. But on
they go. The put-downers. Of which I mercifully
have never been one. So it doesn't make sense. It
just doesn't make sense. I know it's going to happen
and nothing's ever stopped it happening, but it just
doesn't make sense. It's so – so unjust. No reason for
it. I mean what've I done to have all those bloody
marvellous things taken away from me? What?
What, what, what for Christ's sake? (*Pause.*) Daft
bugger, me!

> *MAURICE finds the outburst unbearable.*

> *VICTOR gives him a letter on blue paper to read.
> Turns away.*

SCENE 15

The kitchen.

*SONIA is deftly and lovingly preparing a jar of fresh fruit
slices for VICTOR. (For precise movements see note at end
of play.)*

SONIA (VO) You took me and you shaped me and you gave me
form. Not a form I couldn't be but the form I was
meant to be. You needed only to be in the house and
I felt my life and the lives of the children I cherished
could never go wrong. It was so. They never did go
wrong. They have confidence and pity and daring in
them. And in me there are flowers. Blossoming all
the time. Explosions of colour and energy. You see it,

surely? Surely you see it? Or feel it? There's nothing I couldn't do. In me is you. All you've given me. I've been a white sheet, a large white canvas and you've drawn the world upon me, given outline to what was mysterious and frightening in me. Do you know how proud I've been of you? Do you know I've felt myself beautiful only because you chose me? Do you know that I've shuddered with pleasure to think you love me? You are my rock my hero my love. I feel such strength. Do you know these things?

SCENE 16

Hospital bed.

VICTOR now has a blood-drip attached to his arm, he's very much weaker.

MAURICE sits beside him.

VICTOR Have to renew it every three hours. Stop the flow and I die. Look at it! A bottle of someone else's blood, just that red stuff in there to keep me able to see you and talk and think…and remember and reason.

He shifts a little.

Bloody bedsores. I've got a rubber ring under my backside but it makes no odds. Lying horizontal still stops the blood circulating.

Pause.

This is it, Maurice, isn't it? Oh, don't protest, lad. I don't think I mind now all that much. Like your mother. I understand her. In fact, I've got back me curiosity.

Pause.

You know what helped? I woke-up the other day and suddenly out of the blue, no connection with anything, I thought: Leonardo Da Vinci is dead. And that seemed reassuring. So I went on: Mozart is dead. Socrates is dead, Shakespeare, Buddha, Jesus, Gandhi, Marx, Keir Hardie – they're all dead. And one day Sonia will die. And my son, Graeme, he'll be dead, and my daughter Hilda, and their son, Jake, and so will all the grandchildren... And there seemed a great unity to it all. A great simplicity. Comforting.

> *VICTOR observes how distressed MAURICE is. Offers a reassuring smile and hands him a letter on blue paper.*

VICTOR   Poor Maurice. Here.

SCENE 17

SONIA (VO)   Oh my beloved, my dearest dearest one. I have adored you. Do you know that? That I am full of you – do you? Know it? Know it? That I feel you there as I've felt my children in me, your blood in my blood, rivers of you, do you know it? Do you? Do you?

> *VICTOR's bedroom.*
>
> *A lost, lonely SONIA looks around for what to do.*
>
> *Slowly turns back a corner of the bedcover, as though preparing the bed for the return of its occupant.*
>
> *Achingly she moves from one pointless tidying action to the next, during which –*

The sound of your voice, your judgements, your praise, your love, your pity – all in me, do you know it? My darling, oh my darling. Nothing has been wrong for me and nothing will be. I will give you my everything, cut from me my everything – all my body's everything. To flow in you...

What nonsense do I write instead of just 'I love you and I have always loved you'? But I must catch up on too much silence. So this nonsense, this silliness, this too-much-writing-and-talking-and-shouting is all for you because I can trust it all and anything to you. Don't you know now what I feel? Can't you feel what I feel, mad old woman that I am now? Can't you understand I'd rip myself apart for you, oh my beloved, oh my sweet sweet sweetest one. Why am I so clumsy, never graceful as you deserved. Wretched body, wretched heart, dull old mind not any part of me good enough for you I know but oh I love you love you love you oh my Victor Victor, love you, Victor, love you, oh my Victor my heart.

She has stopped by the framed Ruskin.

Can hold back no longer. Weeps.

SCENE 18

Hospital bed.

VICTOR lies still, staring into space.

MAURICE at his side, leaning forward, head in hands, elbows on knees.

This image, of friend in attendance to dear friend, is held for many seconds, until –

SONIA (VO) There will be, my darling one, I know it, a blinding light –

> *MAURICE starts up, stands, looks at VICTOR, touches his face.*
>
> *VICTOR is dead.*
>
> *MAURICE takes his friend's hand, sits, and presses it to his lips.*

> *Lounge.*
>
> *SONIA is putting on a black coat. Ties a black silk scarf over her head, picks up a holdall, moves to hospital bed. She knows.*
>
> *MAURICE rises to her. Both, either side of the bed, look down on at the prone body.*

SONIA gathers his belongings, folding each item very carefully. Shirt, trousers, jacket, cardigan, tie, socks, shoes…and places them in the holdall.

Kisses him, closes his eyes.

During which…

SONIA (VO) (*Continuing.*) – a painful light when suddenly the lie will fall away from truth. Everything will make its own and lovely sense, trust me, trust me. It won't be logical or happy, this sense, but clear. Everything will become clear. Trust me. Contradictions won't cease to be contradictions, I don't say that, but nor will they any longer confuse. I'm not promising all will seem to have been good, but evil won't bewilder you as it once did. Trust me, I adore you. And with this blinding light will come an ending to all pain. The body's pain the heart's pain the pain in your soul. All in a second. Less than a second. Less than less than a second, I'm sure of it. That's how it will be for us all, I've always known it. No matter how it happens to us. Accident, torture…suddenly at the top of our energies, quietly in bed there will come this flash, this light of a colour we've never seen before. It's a glorious moment beloved. Even for the simpleton, even for him, his foolishness falls away just as from the madman his madness falls away. In the instant they know death so they know truth. In the blinding light of truth they know death. One and the same. I promise you, trust me, love oh my love oh my Victor oh my heart.

Fade out.

Appendix

CUTTING THE FRUIT

A board, a large, very sharp knife, a bowl and large oranges. The fruit is laid on its side, topped, swivelled round, the other end topped. Then it's stood on its end and the knife is run in a curve from the top to the bottom, judging the cut to slice off both the peel and the inner skin. After the first slice it's easy to see where the next cut should come. When all the peel is off then the ribbing, between which each segment of fruit sits, can be seen. The fruit is lifted into one hand on its side and the knife used to cut down alongside each rib of inner skin so that each segment comes cleanly away into the bowl, leaving the skeleton of the skin. Squeeze the remaining juice into the bowl. Practice will make perfect. The actions must be swift from expertise. Confident. The knife must be sharp. The oranges must be large. Some oranges are better for this operation than others. To make the scene compelling it is worth looking for the right orange.

NOTES ON THE LETTERS

Here are my reasons for conceiving the letters as voiceover and not spoken by the actress. Sonia's letters are unexpected. They must surprise us. It must not seem possible that such a woman could be writing them. This dichotomy is central to the play and should be emphasised. Sonia should be engrossed in the details of keeping the house functioning while her other persona emerges through the letters. The character and the first letter are like strangers. As the play evolves, they move closer together to become, magnificently, one and the same. There are two other reasons for the actress not speaking the letters: to look for actions to be silently carried out, to fill the stage with a mute but living presence is a greater challenge for both actress and director. Besides, an element of the absurd occurs if the actress has to deliver the last three letters live, especially the final one which would end being addressed to her husband who lies dead before her.

A word about their rendering. A rough guide is that we are hearing the letters as though she had written them and was now reading them back to herself aloud. Therefore they are more radio than theatre. They come through with more simplicity than theatricality. Punctuation should be carefully followed to achieve the rhythm of their construction. This is not to say they must be delivered blandly but more for their narrative than their emotion. Emotion, as we know, follows from meaning.

The exceptions are the last three letters which take off and possess a greater degree of intensity. But even then only one of them, the penultimate one, moves into pure emotion. In this one, and this one only, Sonia loses control. Not that she weeps her way through the entire letter – she weeps only at the end – but the words flow very swiftly, tumbling out. It is the one time that the 'centre does not hold'. So, the last three letters could be described thus: first – calm but urgent; the second – spinning out of control; the last – strength returned, magnificent, regal.

LADY OTHELLO

Characters

STANTON MYERS
44, professor of American literature, British,
Jewish

ROSIE SWANSON
30, about to become a student, New York,
Catholic, black

STELLA-BELLA
30 to 35, New York Jewish, bony, not beautiful
but not plain; a dropped-out J.A.P. working as a
waitress

FRANCESCA
40, restaurant owner

JUDITH'S VOICE
English

DAUGHTER'S VOICE
English

DELI SHOP ASSISTANT

MAN
Stella-Bella's fella for the night

WOMAN
'Miss Minnelli', outside Sardi's, a customer

and

VOICES

Time

New York. 1976.

Note

This is a play for three actors. The actress playing STELLA-BELLA can also play FRANCESCA, DELI SHOP ASSISTANT, DAUGHTER'S VOICE and WOMAN, thus commanding the talent of a first-rate actress. STELLA-BELLA's fella makes a brief, fifteen-second appearance and can be played by a stage manager. All the VOICES off except one can be played by stage managers or can be recorded. One VOICE off is a central role and must be recorded by, preferably, a well-known actress. This is the voice of STANTON's wife, JUDITH.

Act One

House lights fade. Sound of a Boeing jumbo jet in flight fades up and retreats.

In the darkness:

JUDITH (VO) By the way, did your father tell you he was going to New York to give a lecture?

DAUGHTER (VO) (*Cheerfully.*) No, he's not. He's going to see his girlfriend. Stop him.

JUDITH (VO) Will you not suggest crazy things like that. They upset me.

DAUGHTER (VO) How long's he going for?

JUDITH (VO) Twelve days.

DAUGHTER (VO) Twelve days to give a lecture? Mother!

SCENE 1

Aeroplane toilet.

STANTON finishing shaving with old-fashioned cut-throat. Dangerous! Probably belonged to his father. He's a professor of American literature; handsome, wry, gentle, confident by nature. When finished he puts on a black rollneck sweater. Till then –

STANTON Repeat after me: this relationship can't possibly work because, one: when I'm sixty she will be forty-six. Two: New Yorkers, bless them, are *afflicted* with democracy and feel it a duty to have opinions about everything! Three: she *has* to be right. Four: she doesn't converse, she lectures, too ardently, too often, too loudly and in public places. Five: seems unable to distinguish between disagreement and hostility, rational exchange difficult therefore. Six:

she's never on time, imagines punctuality is a sign of servility. Seven: she's combative, competitive, possessive and contrary. Eight: she has a therapist. And nine: I love my family. (*Pause.*) I must be mad! (*Pause.*) Then why, Professor Stanton Myers, are you travelling three thousand miles to be with a woman who is so utterly not your type? (*Pause. Beaming.*) Because one: I may be wrong. Because two: she's breathtakingly beautiful. Because three: she's sunny. Because four: she's perceptive, supportive, positive and loyal. Because five: her New York humour is irresistible, outrageous, rich, and infectious. Because six: she's powered by an apparently endless and delightfully unashamed lust and I have come to put myself at risk!

SCENE 2

STANTON asleep in aeroplane seat.

Gentle voice of his wife, JUDITH. It is the letter she's written to him before leaving.

JUDITH (VO)　'My darling. All my instincts are to fight tooth and nail to keep you as part of our family but the situation calls for civilised behaviour, doesn't it? Forgive my outbursts, they'll get less and less the more I gain self-control. I do so want you to carry a graceful and dignified image of me. You *must* go to New York, I understand that, I'd hate you as a tormented man, and *if* you come back we'll be here, waiting for your old self to return. The days will get tense from now on with *your* excitement at going and *my* sadness at seeing you go. Be strong, and go knowing that mine is a long-standing love. I'm afraid you'll have to arrange your own luggage, forgive me for not driving you to the airport.'

SCENE 3

Kennedy Airport, arrivals.

STANTON in well-cut brown tweed suit, a black, military-style raincoat over his arm. He's jetlagged.

ROSIE, made up, stunning, radiant, expectant, eager. It is autumn. She wears an old 1930s astrakhan coat with fur collar; beneath it a blue denim skirt and black rollneck sweater. She's a little plump, she's offbeat, she's a beautiful Jamaican-black New Yorker – a kind of Barbra Streisand.

They stand a long moment taking each other in. Strangely shy. He's besotted. She offers him a cheek to kiss, and three roses.

ROSIE   Tired, huh?

STANTON   Deliciously.

ROSIE   Flight wasn't late as you feared.

STANTON   I had to alert you though.

ROSIE   All you had to do was move heaven and earth to get here. I'll provide hell.

STANTON   Don't make jokes. (*Beat.*) Yes, make jokes.

ROSIE   Honey? You sound tired and in need of love and comfort.

STANTON   I don't need love and comfort. I need *you*!

ROSIE   Same thing.

STANTON   (*Playing the professor.*) Not so. Love and comfort I can get from lots of people. *You* I can get from no one.

ROSIE   Shithead!

SCENE 4

Airport coach into New York.

*ROSIE chatters at a ferocious rate, which she does well, fluently
and frequently.*

ROSIE   And then Stella-Bella, my flatmate, rings up from
downstairs by the porter's desk and says, 'Rosie, it's
here, didn't you see it?' And I say, 'What's here?'
'Your results, dumb-dumb,' she says. 'An envelope,
here, with a university's name on it.' 'Stella-Bella,' I
say, 'you've forgotten what time it is. I haven't even
brushed my teeth yet' – because sometimes as a
waitress she's on early shifts for breakfasts and gets
back around ten, ten-thirty, and maybe I've had a
late night cos sometimes I do late shifts in the same
restaurant to subsidise the lousy alimony cheque I
get from my cautious, anxious, mean-as-arsehole ex-
husband, and I say to her, 'Stella-Bella,' I say, 'now
you come straight up with that envelope because
I'm in no fit state to leave this flat and I don't care
how late you are this is life or death for me.' And
she was kinda eager herself to know, was I going to
be allowed entry into the hallowed halls and groves
of academe for a second chance in life or not, so she
rushes up shrieking, 'I'm late! I'm late!' and I tell
her, 'Stella-Bella, pray! I'm opening the envelope,
pray!' Which she did. Stood there like a madonna
– a Jewish madonna, you understand, because with
a name like Stella-Bella she couldn't come from
Neapolitan Catholic stock, you know what I mean?
And she prayed. In Hebrew! 'Stella-Bella,' I said,
'do you know what you're saying because I don't
want you mumbling the incomprehensible to the
Almighty…'

STANTON   Rosie, did they or did they not accept you?

ROSIE   They accepted me!

STANTON   Congratulations!

ROSIE   So now I'll study for a degree in political science by
        day and attend your lectures by night.

        *It's her way of sounding out if he's staying or not. He
        avoids the hidden question.*

STANTON   Why should you attend my lectures on modern
          American literature? You have greater authorities
          than me in NYC.

          She can't stop gazing at him.

ROSIE   Oh, those lips. I've made a list of all the landmarks
        where I want those lips to kiss me.

STANTON   Can't wait.

ROSIE   New York landmarks, dumb-dumb. Jesus, don't look
        at me that way or I'll have to drag you under the seat
        here and now.

STANTON   (*Sinking.*) Drag me.

ROSIE   Sit up and behave. I want to be kissed on Staten
        Island ferry, in Times Square, on a buggy ride
        through Central Park, in a box in a theatre, on top of
        the Twin Towers, in the middle of a disco floor, in –

STANTON   How about in an airport bus?

          *She's been holding back for she knew not what or
          when but now no longer can. Closes her eyes. It's
          their first kiss, and lasts a long time. She wants to
          withdraw, he slaps her 'pushing hand' away, holds
          till she's breathless.*

ROSIE   That what you came all the way from London for, to
        choke me to death? Get it over quickly?

STANTON   Why don't I just chew on your mouth for the rest of
          the journey? It'll give me pleasure and your mouth a
          rest.

ROSIE   (*Quick tempered.*) Don't you get fresh with me.

STANTON   Oh? Guard my English banter, must I?

          *He retreats. A dangerous moment. First-encounter
          nerves. He reaches into a pocket.*

Here, a present for you.

ROSIE   Wait! Let me give you mine first. As they're nothings it'll be less embarrassing that way round.

STANTON   What makes you think mine is 'something'?

ROSIE   I expect you to have brought me the Crown Jewels. Here.

> *She rummages in her large floppy bag and offers him, one by one, five little packages, each neatly wrapped and bowed, evidence of time spent on them.*

> *He unpacks them one by one.*

STANTON   A miniature pack of cards! Of movie stars! What I've always wanted. *Street Cries and Rhymes of New York.* Wow! *The Jewish Connection – Amazing Jewish Achievements.* Only in New York. *Ours Is A Strange And Wonderful Relationship – A Book For Friends, Lovers, And Other Strange And Wonderful People.* (*The fifth is –*) Writing paper!

ROSIE   But you won't need that now cos you're gonna stay with me for ever, aren't you?

STANTON   (*Evading her question.*) I love them all.

> *He withdraws his present – an old Victorian silver locket on a chain. She puts it round her neck, slips her arms through his, cuddles up.*

And I've discovered a new piece of music by Bach which I can't wait to play you. C P E Bach, that is, not J S. The son, not the father. His *Magnificat.*

> *She is very happy.*

SCENE 5

ROSIE's apartment. This will be the main setting.

Hall, lounge/dining room, kitchen – partly visible. Bathroom/ toilet – partly visible. Two doors leading to bedrooms – not visible. One bedroom is rented to STELLA-BELLA. The other belongs to ROSIE's son. ROSIE sleeps on a divan in the lounge which opens out into a double bed.

Her apartment is – well – not filthy, cluttered rather. She's indifferent to 'things'. Records, mostly out of their sleeves, are scattered around. Scant furniture. The divan is in a recess. A round table with four chairs. A couch, armchair, chest of drawers. A wall of shelves filled mostly with books. Cushions on the floor.

ROSIE's in the kitchen preparing a meal. The rest of the apartment is in shadow.

STANTON sprawled out asleep on the floor among the cushions. A record of Jane Olivor's 'First Night' plays softly in the background. The front door opens violently.

ROSIE (*Whispering.*) That you, Stella-Bella?

STELLA-BELLA (*Too loudly.*) That's me, Rosie.

ROSIE Shusssh. You bought yourself Chinese takeaway to eat in your *own* room tonight?

STELLA-BELLA (*Good-tempered patience.*) I bought Chinese takeaway like you said, Rosie, and I'll eat it in my own room like you ordered, Rosie, and you won't know I'm alive, like you want, Rosie.

ROSIE Good girl. Now go and say hello to Stanton and don't maul him around too much cos I haven't unwrapped him yet.

STELLA-BELLA, arms full, moves to front room. She kneels to STANTON and showers him with loud kisses on his face, neck, chest, pausing in between to say:

STELLA-BELLA Rosie said not to maul you around too much.

She continues kissing.

STANTON Stella-Bellaaah! (*Please.*)

STELLA-BELLA Okay! Okay! I'll continue in the morning.

Retires to her room.

ROSIE tiptoes back and forth laying the table, setting up candles, arranging a cheese board. The phone rings. She rushes to grab it.

ROSIE (*Whispering.*) Oh hi, Merle. Yes. He's here. What
d'you mean, how do I feel? I feel like a lump of jelly,
that's how I feel. I feel like I'm back at college with
a crush on my lecturer, which is what's happened
of course, only now I'm a mother! No, we haven't
talked yet. What chance have we had? This guy flew
in a couple of hours ago, did Mark's homework then
zonked out. And I'll tell you something else, buster,
I'm not letting him talk tonight either. This lascivious
woman has other plans for the English gentleman's
native tongue. Mark's with his friend, Stella-Bella's
got Chinese takeaway and a Gary Cooper movie,
and that leaves me the professor and a free lounge
and I tell you neither his views on modern American
literature nor my views on everything are gonna
be taking the floor tonight because I tell you – he is
more beautiful than I remembered and I'm more
in love than I knew was possible so if you want
news about how my future looks you'd better hang
up now and don't call us we'll call you. Do I make
myself plain or do you want me to repeat all that?
(*Long listening pause.*) Oh, Merle, that's awful. I didn't
know your father had gone into hospital. Yeah – sure
sixty is young these days. Keep me in touch. Byeee!

*She lights candles. Pulls down blinds. Changes record
to Johnny Mathis – 'The First Time Ever I Saw Your
Face', and kneels beside the sleeping STANTON. He is
snoring ever so lightly.*

Honey. You're snoring.

He opens his eyes. Smiles.

Don't you *ever* wake troubled?

STANTON I feel loved, why should I wake troubled?

ROSIE Me, I shoot up straight, usually out of a nightmare
– zonk! Like that! My fists ready.

STANTON I love your lies.

ROSIE And I love your lips.

She kisses him.

STANTON You, candlelight, smell of food, Frank Sinatra, what more could a man want?

ROSIE It's Johnny Mathis.

STANTON You, candlelight, smell of food, Johnny Mathis, what more could a man want?

ROSIE Come.

> *She pulls him up, seats him at the table, tucks napkin under his chin.*

Don't you go anywhere, now.

> *Alone, his face changes. Sombre. What a fraught situation.*

> *She returns, catches his expression. In one hand is the dish of kedgeree; in the other, plates with a foil-ful of spare ribs on top.*

> *He rises quickly to take the plates with his napkin – he had thought they were hot. Feels one with the flat of his hand. They're not.*

ROSIE Something wrong?

STANTON Reflex. My hand automatically feels to see the plate's hot.

ROSIE (*Hint of pique.*) Don't heat plates in *this* house, honey.

STANTON Grounds for divorce.

ROSIE (*Quick-tempered.*) You want to ring now see if there's a flight out tonight?

STANTON (*Slowly, calmly.*) Rosie, can we agree on something? Let's give each other's humour space? I can take any amount of crude New York banter from you because you love me and therefore I trust it. I'm Jewish. The Jews take on the personality of the countries in which they find themselves. English Jews are frightfully English, French Jews are (*French accent.*) elegantly French; German Jews, (*German accent.*) zoes who are left, are fearfully Deutsch. Only in New York has it gone the other way, all New Yorkers are

very Jewish. My humour is English – wry, teasing,
sardonic. I love you therefore trust it.

She's just gazing at him.

ROSIE Would you mind saying all that again. You English!
How come you speak the language so beautifully?

STANTON Can I have my spare ribs, please?

*Holding his gaze she reaches for spare rib, offers to his
mouth, he bites, she bites, offers it to him again, pulls
it away, smears his lips with it then tongues the grease
off his lips, melting into a kiss.*

Let me play you the Bach *Magnificat.*

ROSIE Wrong moment.

She continues with the passionate kiss.

*Thus locked they rise from the table, stagger to the
cushions on the floor where he showers kisses on her
face, ears, neck, beneath which she writhes until –*

Fuck the chicken kedgeree.

– and she zips down the zipper of her skirt.

SCENE 6

*ROSIE's apartment next morning. She's on a hands-free
phone.*

*Dressed in an old dressing-gown and wearing glasses she's
putting her hair in curlers. It's as though she's daring
STANTON to love her in any state. It's not difficult. Her sunny
personality shines through.*

ROSIE Yes, Ma, of course he's here. The English are always
on time, didn't you know? Frightened they'll lose
out on something. (*Pause.*) In the kitchen washing up.
What else did I bring him over for? You know me.
(*Pause.*) Yes, yes, you'll get to see him but I'd better
warn you – he's heavy. Yeah, heavy, you know,
Marx, Freud, Woody Allen – that crowd.

*STANTON appears from kitchen with a handful of soap
suds which he pushes inside her gown on her breast.*

Ow! Don't *do* that! (*Pause.*) No, of course not you,
mother. It's this Englishman here, he's getting fresh.
Still thinks we're a colony. (*Pause.*) I'll explain some
other time. Ma, I must go. And listen, here's the bad
news – you're gonna be seeing a lot of Mark over
the next ten days. (*Pause.*) Yeah, I thought you'd hate
that. Bye, Ma. Take care.

*She looks at her watch. Too late to put in any more
curlers. Bunches rest of her hair into an elastic band.
Puts on record of Stevie Wonder, sits on the floor and
commences stretch exercises to the musical rhythm.*

STANTON appears. Watches her.

STANTON Any other woman wearing curlers I'd walk out on.

ROSIE (*Puffing.*) Love me, love my curlers. Did you know
I'd planned to meet you at the airport in curlers?
Curlers and glasses. And then I planned to call your
name loud, kiss you long, and unzip your hide-and-
seek. What would you have done?

STANTON Pretended it wasn't happening, that I didn't know
you. (*Beat.*) Or call the police.

ROSIE Shithead!

STANTON (*With mock earnestness.*) Will you always call me that,
please?

ROSIE (*Pausing in her exercises.*) Tell me, how did you leave
London?

STANTON Sadly.

ROSIE I mean, who knows? Who said what?

*She flops to her back, exhausted and preparing herself
for the worst.*

STANTON can't resist and dives to her side.

Don't get too near, I smell all sweaty.

Which seems not to worry him. Sniffs her like a dog.

STANTON   Mmm!

ROSIE   (*Tenderly.*) Tell me.

> *STANTON sits up, away from her.*

STANTON   My sister said: 'It's because your mother died last
year. You're an orphan!' Our friend, Julie, said: 'It's
passion – passion lasts six months then it's over,
done.' Another friend urged me to talk to another
friend who's a psychiatrist who said: 'She's the
personification of the American literature you love.'
Well, they could all be right, but it struck me, I fall in
love and immediately everyone thinks I'm unwell.

ROSIE   And Judith?

STANTON   Judith runs the house, guards the children, who
guard her. They write witty encouraging notes to
each other and leave them on the table. They are
– waiting.

> *JUDITH'S VOICE takes over.*
>
> *STANTON's finger traces the back of ROSIE's hand but
> a distance is kept as all her female antennae are out.*

JUDITH (VO)   (*Quiet, sad.*) Stanton. I'd like us to talk. Why is it,
do you think, that wives can't be mistresses, or
husbands be lovers? Is it bed? It can't be only that.
A strong element, maybe, but not *only*. Am I keeping
you awake? I'm afraid I'm going to keep you
awake for as long as I can every night until you go
– talking, kissing, touching, remembering. You won't
deny me that, will you, that I send you off as full of
me as she sent you back full of her? I wish you hated
me, I'd understand then, but I know you don't.
How could you hate harmless, loving, wise, playful,
faithful li'l ole me? So tell me. Why can't wives be
mistresses?

ROSIE   And *did* you tell her?

STANTON   I don't want to talk about it.

ROSIE   Tell *me* then. Why can't wives be mistresses?

STANTON   Oh, I don't know. Wives can't be surprised. For a
mistress everything's a surprise. You need to look
into a woman's eyes and see that you're fresh, a
delight for her, you need to catch her looking at you
with expectation. Married couples make each other
feel stale, predictable. In love – your nerve-ends are
charged.

ROSIE   Dammit, Stanton! I don't want to be your mistress. I
want to be your wife.

> *The declaration disturbs him. He can't keep it out of his
> eyes. Nor does she miss it. She leaps up to the bathroom
> – an incredible female mess – and makes up.*
>
> *STANTON follows, leans against the door frame,
> watching, mesmerised. The ritual of contact lenses,
> spitting on make-up boxes, the order of creams, the
> different thicknesses of sticks of eye make-up – all
> fascinate him. She has a rhythm. It's compelling.*
>
> *After a while –*

Stop watching. Makes me nervous.

STANTON   Let me. I love watching you.

> *She continues. But silence is not her territory.*

ROSIE   My therapist says –

STANTON   How can you afford a therapist? Chicken feed
for alimony, *some*times Social Security, *some*times
waitressing –

ROSIE   He's a nice guy. Likes me. He knows he'll get it
sooner or later. So anyway he says, 'Now, Rosie,'
he says, 'you do realise you're entering a classic
situation, don't you?' 'Hell, Mr O'Conolly – ' he's
Irish –

STANTON   There are Irish therapists in New York?

ROSIE   Shut up and listen, will you? 'Hell, Mr O'Conolly,'
I say, 'not only am I entering into a classic situation
I swore I'd never ever let myself get into, but *I* was
the one who got morally outraged when any of my
friends involved themselves with married men.

"That's a disgusting thing to do," I'd tell them.' Jesus look at me…

STANTON   Can't take my eyes off you.

ROSIE   …not only is he married and got children but he's *happily* married. Though I don't know how a man can be happily married and sleep around with a black woman.

STANTON   Are you black?

ROSIE   Well, it sure ain't Californian suntan.

He leans down to kiss her neck, lightly. She freezes with ecstasy. He moves up, kiss by kiss, to her ear. When he moves to her cheek she backs away.

You'll make me late for my swimming lesson, Stanton.

He persists. They embrace.

God! But you're a creep, Stanton.

STANTON   Shithead, please.

ROSIE   Go understand an Englishman! Shithead!

SCENE 7

A coffee shop.

ROSIE is writing out cards fast, furiously, silently. They've quarrelled.

STANTON is appealing.

STANTON   But the streets of New York are paved with gold and jet and garnet and topaz and –

ROSIE   You don't look at other women when you're with me!

STANTON   (*Refusing to take it seriously.*) Who can resist?

ROSIE   First you make me late for swimming, then you spend time gawking at the other swimmers.

STANTON (*Warningly.*) Rosie –

    ROSIE Don't Rosie me.

STANTON Rosie, I'm too old to be chastised.

    ROSIE You're too old to be philandering but you're
philandering!

STANTON (*Lecturer's sternness.*) Don't play Lady Othello, Rosie.

    ROSIE Rub me the wrong way and I'll give you an Othello
undreamt of by Mister Shakespeare.

STANTON It's not just New York girls upsetting you, is it?

    ROSIE You know? Why ask! Now leave me be, I want to
catch the midday mail.

STANTON Christmas cards! It's only the end of November. And
so many?

    ROSIE I like keeping in touch and being kept in touch with.

STANTON (*Trying to change the mood.*) Don't let's play Othello,
Rosie. He was a fool. Shakespeare made a fool of the
black man, and a monster of the Jew. Play Rosalind,
I'll be your Orlando, you'll have the epilogue.

    ROSIE (*Dangerously.*) '…if I once stir, or do but lift this arm,
the best of you shall sink in my rebuke…' Take
me seriously, Stanton, I know *Othello* backwards.
(*Offering him stamps.*) Here. Lick these. Be useful
instead of an aggravation.

STANTON (*Licking and sticking.*) You may be able to quote the
play but if you think Othello was noble you don't
know the play. Besides it's Iago's play.

    ROSIE Not in my reading. Othello is a man who gives
himself utterly. Utterly to war, utterly to jealously,
utterly to love. Wouldn't catch him cheating on
Desdemona for a black chick.

STANTON You want sober intellectual exchange or female
backstabbing?

    ROSIE You're right. Sorry. Ignore the second sentence.
'Othello was a man of passion.' Discuss.

STANTON   What passion? 'She loved me for the dangers I had
           pass'd, and I loved her that she did pity them.' He
           tells the sob story of his life as a slave who escapes
           to conquest and fortune, she sobs with pity, he's
           flattered by her admiration, asks her for her hand,
           they marry. Where's the passion?

ROSIE   He braved the anger of her father and the Duke.

STANTON   He braved nothing! He sees her as something
           bought.

           '…come, my dear love,
           The purchase made, the fruits are to ensue,
           The profit's yet to come 'twixt me and you'

           'The profit's yet to come' not 'The *passion's* yet to
           come.'

ROSIE   That's a crude interpretation, Stanton. The passion is
           in his blood. His problem is he's got no language to
           express it.

           'Rude am I in my speech,
           And little bless'd with the set phrase of peace…'

           He's a general, a man of action but he is endowed
           with a mighty magic, I tell you.

STANTON   And I tell you he's only endowed with a mighty
           prick. Iago has a halter round Othello's neck.

           *He imitates Iago holding rope and performs Iago and
           Othello, making Othello a stereotypical black.*

           Iago: Here, boy, growl, be jealous!
           Othello: I will chop her into messes… Cuckold me!
           Iago: Oh, 'tis foul in her.
           Othello: Wid mine officer!
           Iago: That's fouler.
           Othello: Get me some of de poison, Iago, dis night.
           Iago: Do it not with poison, strangle her in her bed,
           even the bed she hath contaminated.
           Othello: Good, good, de justice of it pleases; very
           good.

           Iago snaps his fingers, Othello jumps.

ROSIE   That's sacrilegious! Sacrilegious and offensive!

STANTON   Sacrilegious, offensive, but perceptive.

SCENE 8

Times Square. The 'same-day ticket-sales kiosk'.

ROSIE   Right! Here's the first landmark.

STANTON   Is this the best spot? I mean can enough people see
            us from here? How about out there? In the middle.
            We can be seen by the traffic going both ways then.

            *ROSIE grabs him. They kiss. Long and passionately
            to the hoots and honks of passing cars.*

ROSIE   Thank you. Now, you wanna book for the theatre?

STANTON   Not really.

ROSIE   What the hell you to mean, Stanton? Everyone goes
            to the theatre in New York.

STANTON   Except intelligent people.

ROSIE   I dare you to stand up on Broadway and say that.

STANTON   Here will do. (*Coughs.*) Good afternoon, ladies and
            gentlemen...

ROSIE   Oh no, Stanton, I wasn't serious.

STANTON   ...I'm a professor of American literature at London
            University and I've been asked to address you today
            on the demise of the Broadway theatre...

ROSIE   Christ Almighty! These fucking Englishmen!

STANTON   ...I would put it to you, ladies and gentlemen of the
            New York theatre-going public, that when people
            enter the theatre they lower their intellectual and
            emotional expectations and accept a level of infantile
            relationships and utterances that no publisher of
            Bellow, Updike, Wharton, Roth, Ozick, Doctorow,
            Jong, would contemplate for one moment offering a
            reading public. It is to the American novel that we
            must turn for any serious intellectual or emotional
            stimulation...

ROSIE   Stanton! Oh, Jesus Christ! Are you crazy? In my
            own city? How do you expect me to walk these
            streets again? You want to spend these next eleven
            days in jail?

STANTON   I don't think I really mind where I have you as long
            as I have you.

ROSIE   Honey, we don't have mixed jails here yet.

            *STANTON looks down the list of theatre tickets
            available.*

STANTON   No Miller, no Williams, no O'Neill, no Albee, no
            Gelber, no Kopit – ha! *Othello*!

            A mischievous grin. Then –

            What? Twenty-five dollars each! *That's* half price?
            Twenty-five bloody dollars each?

ROSIE   This is Broadway nineteen hundred and seventy-six,
            honey.

STANTON   That's two days' pay. That's twenty breakfasts, half a
            dozen novels and fifteen films. No play can be worth
            that.

ROSIE   Buy!

SCENE 9

*FRANCESCA's restaurant. After the play. Waiting to be
served.*

STANTON   Everyone in that play is a fool. Iago succeeds in
            duping Othello, Desdemona, even his own wife!
            'A man he is of honesty and trust…honest Iago,'
            cries Othello. 'Oh that's an honest fellow,' cries
            Desdemona. 'Good madam… I know it grieves my
            husband, as if the case were his,' cries Iago's wife.
            Villainy rings in every syllable of Iago's speech and
            no one notices!

ROSIE   (*Gazing adoringly.*) I could listen to you speaking
            English all day.

STANTON I mean Othello's a general of men, he's supposed to be able to see through his opponents in war yet he can't see through this transparent knave. Who could believe such a nincompoop capable of passion?

ROSIE First of all there's no relationship between a power of perception and the possession of passion.

STANTON (*Genuinely.*) Oh, I like that. A very succinct formulation.

ROSIE You want sober intellectual exchange or you want to trade put-downs.

STANTON But I meant it! Kiss me!

ROSIE Anyone ever tell you you were a shithead?

STANTON No one's ever loved me enough!

ROSIE (*Throwing screwed-up bread at him.*) Shithead!

> *FRANCESCA, the owner, approaches.*

STANTON Hello, Francesca. You probably don't remember me but about two months ago I was giving a series of lectures and I used to come here –

FRANCESCA You don't have to remind me. You're the English professor of American literature. Right?

ROSIE (*Impressed.*) Right.

> *FRANCESCA to ROSIE.*

FRANCESCA Who could forget a voice like that.

ROSIE I keep telling him but he thinks it's just flattery.

STANTON This is my friend, Rosie.

FRANCESCA Nice to know you, Rosie. Welcome.

ROSIE Lovely place you've got here.

FRANCESCA We've got our friends, like this young man –

STANTON Stanton, and no longer young, dammit!

FRANCESCA Stanton-and-no-longer-young-dammit!

STANTON Can we think a little longer?

FRANCESCA Sure. Take your time. The bouillabaisse is very good. And the veal in mozzarella.

STANTON But we *will* have some wine to be getting along with, please. (*To ROSIE.*) White?

ROSIE Depends what I eat.

STANTON I see. It's going to be that kind of evening, is it?

FRANCESCA The lady's right.

STANTON Yes, but I was thinking of just a little starter – like a glass of cold Chablis.

ROSIE (*Cantankerously.*) Prefer red, myself.

STANTON (*Alert to her changing mood.*) I don't imagine that presents a problem. (*To FRANCESCA.*) Do you sell wine by the glass?

FRANCESCA No, but I've just opened a bottle of red for myself and I'd be happy to offer Daisy –

ROSIE Rosie.

FRANCESCA – Rosie, a glass of mine. And there's a nice half bottle of Californian Pouilly-Fuissé in the fridge.

STANTON Splendid! I knew I'd come to the right restaurant.

FRANCESCA leaves.

But have I brought the right guest?

ROSIE What's that supposed to mean?

STANTON You don't prefer red, you prefer white. I remember from last time.

ROSIE Well, I've changed in a couple of months, haven't I?

STANTON No, you are as contrary as ever.

ROSIE (*Sour, but glued to menu.*) Zat's so?

STANTON (*Veering away.*) You didn't finish telling me what *your* friend said.

ROSIE (*Quick-tempered.*) I'd like to concentrate on the menu, do you mind?

He's hurt. Retreats.

I mean I'm a hungry girl, haven't eaten since before
the show. You know me – I don't get to eat when
I need I become neurotic. My therapist says it's
rewards. I'm looking for rewards all the time. I tell
him, 'Rewards for what? I spend most of my time
ashamed for doing nothing, why should I reward
myself?' 'Precisely so, my dear child,' he says. 'The
more you do nothing to earn rewards from society
the more you feel the need to reward yourself!' Neat,
huh? Now I can eat without guilts because I know
why I eat. I feel guilty!

> *STANTON remains unamused. She becomes winningly
> tender.*

Oh, honey, I'm sorry. But I'm getting vibes from
you. You're ill at ease and that makes me ill at ease.
We're gonna have to talk soon, cos I gotta know.

STANTON No one has ever been able to drain me of feeling one
second and fill me the next.

ROSIE Stella-Bella said to me when you left two months
ago: 'Rosie, this is a one off! They don't make
repeats. This one *don't* let get away.'

> *They twist their hands round each other across the
> table. He opens her palm, kisses it, tongues it.*

(*Rising.*) Oh my God! Let's go.

STANTON (*Bringing her down.*) Each appetite in its place.
Choose!

ROSIE (*At him with deliberate ambiguity.*) I've chosen.

SCENE 10

ROSIE's apartment.

*The lovers in bed. Passionate embraces. Candle flickering. Jane
Olivor on the deck. Sound of a key in the front door.*

STANTON What's that?

ROSIE My, you're jumpy. It's only Stella-Bella. Relax.

STELLA-BELLA is trying to tip-toe quietly to her room.

STANTON   I'm not sure I can make love in the middle of a thoroughfare.

ROSIE   Stella-Bella? That you?

STELLA-BELLA   It's me, Rosie. It's me. Go back to sleep or however else you were passing the time. Reading maybe.

STANTON   Not since my student days...

STELLA-BELLA   My student days were never like this. We had to be satisfied with backs of cars and the other girls moaning alongside.

ROSIE   Goodnight, Stella-Bella.

STELLA-BELLA   I didn't make it to a real bed till I was twenty-one.

ROSIE   Goodnight, Stella-Bella.

STELLA-BELLA   And I had to get married for that.

ROSIE   Goodnight, Stella-Bella.

STELLA-BELLA kisses STANTON.

STELLA-BELLA   (*Leaving.*) My first and last marriage. Divorced at twenty-two. I married a teenage mother-freak!

The door slams.

ROSIE returns her attention to STANTON, her hands exploring under the blankets.

STANTON   It's gone, I'm afraid. Took fright. Probably for ever.

ROSIE makes a deep-throated, lascivious growl-cum-uhhh! and sinks under the bedclothes.

And I'll tell you something else. Othello's cruel. Ow! And a hypocrite. Ouch! And dishonest. Oweee!

ROSIE emerges out from under the blankets.

ROSIE   Proof! Evidence!

STANTON   How about this, then. He doesn't kill his wife at once, no! He *announces* he's going to kill her, and then he lets her wait for thirty-three lines to be uttered before he moves in for the strangulation, at which point she begs to be allowed a prayer and he refuses! First he lets her linger with the knowledge of her death and then he denies her soul its peace. Not cruel?

ROSIE   You're a pedant! You don't see the man's passion because you don't understand the nature of passion.

At which point she draws out a gun from under her pillow.

Okay, buster, this is it.

STANTON is genuinely surprised.

STANTON   Rosie?

ROSIE   Stand!

STANTON   (*Braving it.*) Me or him?

ROSIE   You know which one of you I'm talking to.

STANTON   Jesus, Rosie! At my age I'm only supposed to do it once in seven days, not seven times in one day.

ROSIE   Kiss me, then.

He does so.

That wasn't a kiss.

STANTON   Sorry.

She puts away the gun. Sits up in bed.

ROSIE   Okay, let's talk. You've not been a hundred per cent with me since you've arrived. If you've made decisions I want to know what they are.

STANTON   Can I introduce you to the Bach *Magnificat* first?

ROSIE   No mood music. You're on your own.

STANTON   I haven't made decisions. I'm still working out priorities.

ROSIE   Which are?

STANTON   My children. Them I adore above everyone.

ROSIE   Even more important than your whole future?

STANTON   Oh, infinitely.

ROSIE   Then I don't understand why you came back.

STANTON   To put my whole future in danger.

ROSIE   You'd do that?

STANTON   I'm in the grip of a passion, a little crazy. I'm trying to understand.

ROSIE   You mean there's hope for us?

STANTON   I don't know, Rosie, can't you see I don't know? I've fretted and worried and lived through fantasies: me staying now; me coming back in a few months for good; you coming to London; both of us living partly here partly there. But I can't decide. I've come to put myself at risk, stand at the edge, see if I dare jump.

ROSIE   Good! So now I know what's eating you – indecision. I know where I am. I've got ten days to win or lose you. Right?

STANTON   Don't put it like that, you make me sound like a prize.

ROSIE   But you are, honey. In this city, this age, you are a prize and a half. And I'm gonna fight.

Long pause.

Damn you, Stanton! You've embarked me on an academic career which is probably out of my fuckin' reach and filled me full of discontent so I won't ever put up with second best because now I know what's possible you give me a choice of something or nothing and I'll choose nothing and I have to face the prospect you might leave me!

They sit up side by side. She's deep in thought. He's watching her carefully to see which way she'll go.

JUDITH'S VOICE creeps over them.

JUDITH (VO)   It'll be hard for you, Stanton, won't it? You listening or you asleep? It'll be hard. How will you be able to explain that we actually like and respect one another? She *will* think you odd. I mean *I* think you even love me. Poor Stanton, what a dilemma! You won't be able to say any of the traditional things like, 'My wife and I haven't slept together for three years.' Or, 'My wife doesn't understand me.' I mean, how will she be able to love a man who can't complain about his wife? And what about the family network and the friends you cherish and all our rituals of Sunday lunches, and Sunday teas, surprise birthday parties, and the musical Friday evenings? I mean, would she let a quintet of amateur musicians loose in her house playing obscure seventeenth-century music? Hard, Stanton, hard, I *wish* I could help.

ROSIE   Right! Ten days? Boy! Whatever you decide these are going to be ten days *you* will never forget! I'm going to make sure if you leave me that you'll regret this decision for the rest of your fuckin' life.

STANTON   Rosie, that's not the most inviting tone for a love affair that's going to decide our future.

ROSIE   I didn't set it out, you did. Now, on the last evening I want to have half a dozen of my best friends over for dinner to meet you. I promised them.

STANTON   And I'll cook.

ROSIE   You *cook*?

STANTON   Almost cordon bleu.

ROSIE   Oh holy mother of Christ! I may be losing him and he cooks as well! Would you believe my luck!

STANTON   We've got our landmarks to cover, and I want to play you one game of chess in Washington Square and eat one of our desserts at Serendipity, and go to just one concert –

ROSIE   And I want us to go discoing and to a porno movie.

STANTON   A *porno* movie?

ROSIE   I've never been to one and I want to experience it with you. Now, be still and let me read you an Emerson poem.

Reaches for a book.

STANTON I bet I know which one it will be.

ROSIE Which one, smart arse?

STANTON 'Give all to love'.

ROSIE You're too clever for me. Here – (*Gives him book.*)
– you read it to me then.

STANTON 'Give all to love;
Obey thy heart;
Friends, kindred, days,
Estate, good fortune,
Plans, credit and the Muse – nothing refuse.

> *ROSIE begins kissing his body as he reads.*

'Tis a brave master,
Let it have scope:
Follow it utterly,
Hope beyond hope:
High and more high...

> *Her embraces are too much. He snaps book shut,
> stretches, moans...*

SCENE 11

ROSIE's apartment.

*STANTON is making the meal, moving in and out of the
kitchen. ROSIE is ironing. They're in the middle of a heated
discussion.*

STANTON Let us formulate the question simply. Is the play
about Othello's jealousy or about Iago's villainy and
Othello's poor power of judgement?

ROSIE Othello's jealousy.

STANTON But they don't even have a love scene.

ROSIE 'If it were now to die,
'Twere now to be most happy, for I fear
My soul hath her content so absolute,
That not another comfort, like to this

Succeeds in unknown fate…
…it is too much of joy.'

Did *you* ever say such things to me, creep?

STANTON Shithead, please.

ROSIE Shithead?

STANTON A dozen lines of love and that's all.

ROSIE Compose me one such line and I'm yours whatever you or your wife may say, shithead.

STANTON Oh, that name!
'If it were now to die,
'Twere now to be most happy…'

ROSIE (*Throwing things at him.*) Shithead! Shithead! Shithead!

> *ROSIE's reactions are complex. Each time the adrenalin from intellectual skirmishes flows she is reminded that one day soon they may end. STANTON may be gone for ever. Which changes her mood. She becomes mean.*

Well, I must say you disappoint me. I've seen your dilemma a dozen times. Husband hangs on, wife despises him, kids fucked up.

STANTON Rosie, don't. You're being textbook again.

ROSIE Stop putting me down. These are not textbook, they're *my* observations.

STANTON They may be your *experiences* but experiences are not observations.

ROSIE Oh, you and your fucking distinctions.

STANTON Very useful, distinctions. They prevent the successful from imagining they're eminent and the eminent from imagining they're omnipotent.

ROSIE You don't take me seriously.

STANTON I do, Rosie, I do, believe me. But it hurts to hear you trotting out simplistic explanations of complex problems. In my house is love and warmth and comradeship and much joy. *That* is the problem. Grapple with that.

> *It is a problem. One she knows she can't overcome. She becomes cold. He approaches to touch and console her.*

ROSIE   (*Viciously.*) Get your hands off me, mister.

STANTON   Rosie.

ROSIE   I'm so angry. I'm so murderously angry to be at the end of your indecision.

STANTON   I could get a flight back tomorrow?

ROSIE   Please your fucking self.

> *He moves back to the kitchen. She weeps. Then –*

Stanton! Where the hell are you? You come back here and stop leaving me every time I scold you.

> *He returns. They embrace. She takes up ironing. He goes off for a plate of goodies. Offers her a pickled pepper.*

STANTON   Taste.

> *She bites. He bites. He offers her a small meatball.*

Taste.

> *She bites. He bites. He offers her a forkful of cold creamed potatoes with onions.*

Taste.

> *She sucks. He takes the remainder.*

ROSIE   This the way you're gonna feed me all evening?

STANTON   This evening I'm going to serve you and fuss over you like you've never been served and fussed over before.

ROSIE   To make sure I *really* suffer when you go.

STANTON   If I go.

ROSIE   If you go.

He offers her a pickled cucumber, she reaches for it but he pulls it away.

STANTON   When will be the right time for the Bach *Magnificat?*

ROSIE   You'll know.

STANTON   Taste.

She bites. He bites. She returns to ironing. He returns to preparing the meal.

ROSIE   Food! My therapist is right. I'm a pig!

STANTON   Your therapist calls you a pig?

ROSIE   He says I've got an eating problem but he means pig. I'll be all right when we're married. You *are* gonna marry me, aren't you Mister Stanton Myers, sir? Cos you won't find anyone to wait on you, cook for you, care for you, suffer, forgive and adore you as I do. (*Beat.*) To say nothin' of the fuckin'.

STANTON   Rosie, can we last six months together do you think?

ROSIE   Why I thought a thing of beauty was a joy fah iver, Mister Stanton, suh.

STANTON   Things, perhaps. People not.

ROSIE   Why, Mister Stanton! You're a cynic I do declare.

STANTON   Rosie, can we lay Scarlett O'Hara to rest? Tell me what your PhD thesis will be?

ROSIE   Passion! Men are driven by passions. Makes them irrational. The conduct of political affairs is perverted by irrational men. That'll be my thesis. Surprises you, huh? Coming from a woman who's driven by passions which make her behave irrationally?

What follows is calculated to inflame him sexually and impress him intellectually. At the same time.

She undresses and then dresses up in bra, panties, suspenders, stockings and a see-through dress. She does it all casually, far more interested in what she's saying. But in fact it is a strip show. He is mesmerised.

You take protest. Nothing wrong with protest. Sign of a healthy society. What goes wrong? I'll tell you what goes wrong. People! They fuck it up. Start off wanting more democratic rights, end up wanting to overthrow democratic institutions.

You take commerce. People rage against capitalism. Nothing wrong with trading. Healthy instinct. What goes wrong? I'll tell you what goes wrong. People! They fuck it up. Get greedy. Produce cheap goods. Form totalitarian monopolies which become a law unto themselves.

You take politics. Nothing wrong with politics. It's the art of government. We have to be governed. Since Adam! So what goes wrong? I'll tell you what goes wrong. People! They become politicians, fuck up politics. Ambitious! Dishonest! Opportunist!

You take religion. Nothing wrong with wanting to believe in a God. Jesus! Buddha! Muhammad! They're all saying the same thing – be good, love one another, look after the kids! So what goes wrong? I'll tell you what goes wrong. People! They become fanatics. Scream at one another. 'I'm holier than thou and all must be as holy as me!'

You take science. 'Science will blow up the world! Pollute the earth!' Bullshit! You wanna attack Newton, Galileo, Benjamin Franklin? Science gave me my contact lenses and saved Mark dying from diphtheria. So what goes wrong? I'll tell you what goes wrong. People! Along come the crooked industrialists, the dishonest politicians and the righteous fanatics, and *they* fuck up science.

> *She's finished and beams her full power upon STANTON who is sagging.*

Guess I tired you out, huh? And we haven't even started tonight's studies, honey.

> *She nibbles his ear. Tongues it.*

STANTON   Rosie, I don't think I'm gonna make it tonight,
          Rosie…

ROSIE   You're not *what*? Are you talking to *me*? Are you
        saying I can't rouse your banner high?

His neck.

Are you saying there's no arrow for my bull's-eye?

His chest.

Are you suggesting I can't make your fella meet my
requirements? Because I do have requirements, you
know. I'm not just a housewife or a brilliant intellect.
You're sleeping with a creature. A ker-reecha!

*She bites his nipple and slides her hand down to his
crotch.*

Uh-huh! And what have we here? You only use this
thing for stirring yaw tea, honey? You all don't think
I can fall asleep with this piercing my back all night,
do you? It has to be attended to and tamed and I'm
just the kiddy to do it.

She pulls him down to the cushions.

I mean you take sex. There's nothing wrong with s–

*STANTON claps his hand over her mouth then plants
upon her lips a wild kiss.*

Poor, tormented STANTON.

SCENE 12

ROSIE's apartment.

Next morning. Still dark. Hint of dawn. They're in bed.

ROSIE is trying to sleep.

STANTON, roused, is now going to prove insatiable.

ROSIE   Oh no. It's awake. Stanton, how can I be beautiful
        for you if you don't let me get my beauty sleep?
        (*Pause.*) You're an animal, you know that? (*Pause.*) Is
        this a dagger that I feel behind me?

STANTON   Now could I do such things…

ROSIE   Stanton, can I tell you what time it is?

STANTON   What matter the hour, the day, the time, the place…

ROSIE   (*Curling up to sleep again.*) Well, if you're just going to be literary about it…

STANTON   (*Nibbling her between lines.*)
'Pray do not mock me.
I am a very foolish fond old man,
Four score and upward, not an hour more nor less…'

ROSIE   Stanton, could you, me and King Lear get another hour's sleep? We've a swimming lesson this morning.

STANTON   '… And, to deal plainly,
I fear I am not in my perfect mind.'

ROSIE   I'll drown.

Movement in bed.

Jesus! Stanton! You're an animal, you know that?
I think you're a brute, an animal and a sex fiend.
(*Beat.*) And I want you to know I appreciate it. Yes.
Oh my God, yes, yes, yes, yes! Oh my golly God,
Stanton, what the hell are you doing to me? No
one's ever – I mean how – I mean, yes, yes, yes!
Jesus Christ, Stanton, it's eight thirty in the morning,
I've just seen my kid off to school, I haven't read
the papers yet, and I'm coming, I'm coming, I'm
– aaaaaaaah!

Orgasm.

SCENE 13

ROSIE's apartment.

Bright morning.

ROSIE, in a dressing-gown, glasses, reading a newspaper by the breakfast table.

STANTON, opposite her, also in a dressing-gown. He has a strange look in his eyes. He's slowly slipping off his chair and under the table as though dragged. A low-hung cloth hides him.

ROSIE lowers her paper.

ROSIE Stanton, where are you going, Stanton?

She realises where he's going.

Stanton, are you crazy? Stella-Bella could come through at any moment. Get up from there.

But he doesn't. Something is happening. She smiles. Is aghast. Shocked. Delighted.

Stanton, I think you're disgusting. I don't think you're English at all. Stanton, don't *do* that –

But she positions herself to make it easier for him.

– we've just had breakfast, Stanton, my milk will curdle. What's got into you this morning? You're possessed! I mean – oh my God! Again! Stanton, you keep doing this and I'll turn grey. Oh, oh, oh, my Lord. Oh, I don't believe this is happening. I just don't believe this – yes, yes, yes! There! Oh yes, there, there! Oh Lordee – here I come again, before I've had a chance to read the gossip column I'm comin', comin', comin'…aaaaaaaah!

Orgasm.

ROSIE flops over the table. Stillness. Then – from somewhere beneath the table there reaches up to us the defiant – if unskilled – mating call of a Tarzan. Of sorts!

SCENE 14

ROSIE's apartment some minutes later.

ROSIE in the bathroom making up.

STANTON, still in his dressing-gown, still zombie-like, approaches. Takes her arm and pulls her to the wall against which he pins her.

She regards him as though he were a madman. Feigns terror.

ROSIE Ahhh! It's him! The sex-crazed Hebrew from outer space. Stanton, give a girl a break, will ya?

> *To no avail. She's wrenched up and clasped in his arms. The brute!*

Stanton, I've just made up and make-up's expensive and – don't look at me that way. I mean – would you believe this? I mean is this happening?

> *He's covering her with kisses, slowly slithering down her body.*

Stanton, you're beginning to worry me. I mean, one or the other of us is gonna have a heart attack and as I've got fourteen years on you guess which one it's gonna be! And, Stanton, may I remind you your lecture's tomorrow and there's folk expecting serious thoughts from you on American literature?

> *His head is now under, and covered by, her dressing-gown, in the region below her belly.*

Stanton, you're psychotic! You know that? An Anglo-Saxon psychotic. I don't believe I'm in the same world as this occurrence, I just don't. Ah! Ah! Aaaaaaaah!

> *Over which moan we hear the glorious opening 'Magnificat' section of the CPE Bach Magnificat.*
>
> *Blackout.*

Act Two

SCENE 1

C P E Bach Magnificat.

Scenes of New York.

ROSIE and STANTON kissing at each landmark:

Guggenheim Museum

Macy's

Twin Towers

And less familiar landmarks:

Bridle Path Arch Central Park

Flat Iron Building, 167–169 West 23rd Street

Grace's Church in the Village

Finally:

SCENE 2

FRANCESCA's restaurant.

ROSIE and STANTON waiting for their meal. They seem unable to stop touching one another – face, hands, palms, in and out of each others fingers. He is besotted.

STANTON   Ah, Rosie. I'm allowing such powerful needs to enter me now.

FRANCESCA arrives with champagne and pours.

ROSIE   We didn't order champagne, Francesca.

STANTON   Yes we did.

ROSIE   Stanton! You're so extravagant! You won't have enough left to keep me in the style to which you are accustoming me. I mean he doesn't think I'm breaking open my kid's money box for him, does he?

FRANCESCA   Lovers, lovers, lovers! I love lovers.

ROSIE   Another crazy romantic.

FRANCESCA   Some people hate them, you know. Nothing drives
them madder than to see two people kissing. Love's
an affront. You ever thought about that? Love's an
emotion so charged and pure that it can attract a
pure and charged hatred. That's why I don't think
lovers should love in public. Some people have
murder in their eyes when they see lovers but
somewhere out there is a person so disappointed
with their life, so full of self-contempt, they're
carrying murder in their pocket. A gun to blow away
lips that were blowing kisses. (*Imitates a gun.*) Pyeach!
Pyeach! 'Put that tongue back in your mouth, lover!'
Pyeach! Pyeach! 'Put them arms down by your sides,
lover!' Pyeach! Pyeach! 'Wipe that shine from your
eyes, lover! Who gave you the right to be happy
when I'm not?' Pyeach! Pyeach! So drink up, lovers.
Here you can hold hands, gaze at each other, touch
and blow kisses. You're safe. Drink!

FRANCESCA leaves.

But nowhere are they safe from each other.

ROSIE   I'd break open my kid's money box for a man who
was staying *by* me, but for a deserter? Yuk! Cheers!

STANTON   Cheers.

*Her mood, imperceptibly, has changed. FRANCESCA's
speech has reminded her of what she might be losing.*

STANTON doesn't see it for a while.

ROSIE   You buy your wife champagne like this?

STANTON   You really want to know?

ROSIE   Sure! Gotta know the competition. Tell me – she
beautiful? She educated? A raving beauty and a
dazzling intellect? Does she like your friends? Are
they your friends or her friends? Did you meet in
university?

STANTON   (*Sensing the wind.*) Which question first?

ROSIE   You got a *lot* of friends?

STANTON   No, a small circle of friends but a wide circle of
acquaintances.

ROSIE   Open house, huh?

STANTON   It's a large, Jewish family; colleagues from abroad;
kitchen full of children's friends; phone ringing
constantly; steady flow of invitations to lecture in
foreign parts…

ROSIE   You're famous, huh?

STANTON   No, obliging.

ROSIE   So?

STANTON   So what?

ROSIE   Tell me. She beautiful?

STANTON   Rosie, don't.

ROSIE   I'd never run my household the way she runs yours
– all that entertaining. No one, but *no* one except a
special few would ever stay! Jesus! Cleaning up after
house guests? Not this lady. *Your* lady may be a good
little house-lady but not this little lady.

STANTON   Rosie, you're spoiling the mood.

ROSIE   (*Snapping.*) Don't patronise me. I got a right to know
the fuckin' chick I'm competing against.

He's chilled by her crude handling of JUDITH.

STANTON   We're on dangerous ground, Rosie.

Lowers his voice. Other guests are sitting close by.

Especially here.

ROSIE   (*Loud.*) Oh, shucks, Stanton, I gotta right.

STANTON   (*Firmly, in low steady tones, hoping to still her.*) In our
circle she's an anchor. People don't tell her she's
beautiful, they tell her she's radiant. Once a friend
said to her, 'Everyone leaves your house happier.'
There. You asked. And you better know, Rosie, any
tantrum you can manufacture I can match.

FRANCESCA comes with one bowl of chowder soup.

As they spoon together – the fun now gone from the idea – we hear JUDITH'S VOICE.

JUDITH (VO) Stanton, you won't talk to her about me, will you? She'll want to know, but don't. Not only because I don't want you to but because she'll hate you for it. She won't really understand such a set-up – our family, our friends, our children. It'll lead to such wretched moments my darling, believe me, it'll spoil your holiday. Oh, I'm sorry. It's not a holiday, is it? It's a business trip. To discover if you're in love.

By which time they've come to the end of the soup.

STANTON Want the dregs?

ROSIE They're yours.

STANTON You can sip them out, like a cup.

She declines.

He lifts the bowl to his lips.

ROSIE Even on you that looks grotesque.

STANTON You don't mean 'grotesque' you mean 'gross'.

ROSIE (*Viciously.*) *Don't* correct me!

STANTON (*Reflex.*) It's my job to know about words.

ROSIE Fuckin' professors.

STANTON Words are my passion. I make distinctions for my children, and –

ROSIE Well, I'm not one of your fuckin' children.

STANTON (*Anxious about neighbours.*) Rosie, hush.

ROSIE And don't hush me, either! I'm not one of your fuckin' anything.

STANTON Rosie, I may be young at heart but I'm too old for petulance and infantile scenes in public which I hate, just hate. My parents quarrelled in public and public quarrelling mortifies me.

ROSIE Well, ain't that a shame now.

At which she rises, looking for the loo.

(*Gruffly.*)Where is it?

He nods a direction. She leaves.

Though he tries to maintain a cool, controlled stance the scene has unnerved him.

Is this confirmation that their relationship could never work?

FRANCESCA brings the main course. She registers his glum face.

FRANCESCA I never promised you a rose garden.

No response.

Here, take our matches and write something nice on the flap so it's here when she gets back.

STANTON Like what?

FRANCESCA Oh, I don't know. How about 'I love you'?

No response.

Someone has to say it.

She leaves. He writes and places it on top of her chicken.

ROSIE returns. Glares at the propped-up match book. Ungraciously flings it aside.

ROSIE You stuck that thing right in my sauce, you idiot.

STANTON (*With dignity.*) Rosie, I don't enjoy *any*one speaking to me rudely.

ROSIE (*Ignoring that.*) If you love me why are you such a fuck?

STANTON Okay. Let's call a halt, shall we?

She attacks her food but knows she's gone too far.

ROSIE Do you realise you never apologise?

STANTON Because it's always you who starts a quarrel.

ROSIE That's just not possible, Stanton. It takes two to start a fight, it always takes two.

STANTON No. It takes two to become *involved* in a fight, but only one is needed to start it.

ROSIE And what about the conflict between the German people and Hitler which lead to the extermination of the Jews?

>*STANTON is shocked by this non sequitur. It's not the level on which he's used to conducting exchanges.*

STANTON Rosie, what on earth are you talking about? That doesn't make sense.

ROSIE Don't say that!

STANTON And how can you trivialise a monstrous event like the Holocaust by comparing it to our petty squabble?

ROSIE (*Relentless, indifferent to his arguments.*) Because everyone knows the German Jews deluded themselves thinking it couldn't happen to them.

STANTON (*Wanting to end it.*) Okay. I accept that point. I too believed this quarrel couldn't happen to me, and for that reason I'm guilty and contributed to it.

>*He retrieves the match book to tear it up. ROSIE had planned to keep it.*

ROSIE (*Pleading.*) Don't do that, don't tear it up, Stanton.

STANTON (*Continuing.*) That's my mistake, to have stood in line as victim.

>*He rips as ROSIE cries out.*

ROSIE No! No!

STANTON I should not have been there! Now, change the subject.

>*Neither can finish the meal.*

ROSIE You were so quick to tear that up.

STANTON Not true. It was lying around for many minutes. My kind of apology. You rejected it.

>*Silence. She weeps.*

ROSIE   (*Pathetically.*) You have no respect for me, for my opinions, my education, nothing –

But do they both know that was their watershed?

SCENE 3

ROSIE's apartment. Later that evening.

Jane Olivor on the turntable. ROSIE in STANTON's arms on the cushions.

ROSIE   I feel so mediocre. So washed-up and mediocre. University? Me? Huh! That's quixotic for you. (*Pause.*) Shut up being silent, Stanton. It's a sign of superiority, it gets on my nerves, and it isn't helping.

He extends a hand.

Oh, I don't want your fuckin' hand, I want your fuckin' being. All or nothing, me.

At which she lifts his arm and crawls into him.

I've blown it, haven't I?

He makes no response.

What am I gonna do? Jesus Christ, what am I gonna do?

She plies his chest with kisses, reaches his lips, urgently.

He responds, till – slam! The front door!

STELLA-BELLA has entered pushing a young, embarrassed, virginal and terrified man ahead of her.

STELLA-BELLA   (*To them.*) Okay, you two, easy now. You didn't hear me. My hands are full of groceries and I'm a little drunk on account of this fella who's kindly helped me up the lift. (*Whispering to him.*) In there! In there! No, not that door, shmuck, I don't sleep in the bath! (*Back to them.*) So if I've woken you up forgive me; if I've interrupted your conversation that's not, believe me, the end of the world; if I've fucked up your relationship deduct it from my rent! No! That didn't make sense. I pay *you* rent.

(*To MAN.*) Hey, shmuck! Jesus Christ, I wish I could remember his name. Hey, I'm in distress, close the door!

> *Her bedroom door slams.*

> *ROSIE and STANTON lie back. Tension eased.*

STANTON   Which French philosopher, do you think, said: 'Life is like a cucumber; one minute it's in your hand, the next it's up your arse!'?

> *She smiles, snuggles into him. They are happy just to be in each other's arms.*

ROSIE   Okay. Here's what we do. You want to shop for records for your kids? We'll do that in the morning. Lunch and kiss in a little Italian place I wanna show you. Whitney Art Gallery in the afternoon for postcards and more kisses, and then we'll think of some place extraordinary for dinner. Wadja think?

STANTON   Whatever you say, sweetheart.

ROSIE   He called me 'sweetheart'! Oh! I'll die! Call me that again, quick.

STANTON   Call you 'what' again, sweetheart? 'Sweetheart'? I prefer 'Rosie'. You can variate a name like Rosie. My Rose, my Rosebud, my Rosie-lipped, my Rosaline, my Rosamunda, my Rose-of-thorns, my Rosanna. I can sing 'Rosannas' to a Rosie.

ROSIE   (*Kissing him.*) Oh, those lips. What am I gonna do, what am I gonna *do*?

STANTON   Continue plotting.

ROSIE   Right! Tomorrow night's the night!

STANTON   The night?

ROSIE   Porno movie night! At last! Someone I can trust to go with. After which – disco!

STANTON   (*Mock serious.*) Are you absolutely certain you want to go through with this?

ROSIE (*Gazing at him.*) Your lips will be the death of me.

STANTON I need a drink.

> *STANTON, trying always to control the temperature, frees himself and goes to the kitchen.*
>
> *Light from fridge. Sound of pouring. Silence. Sound of running water.*
>
> *ROSIE can't understand what's happening.*

ROSIE What the hell you doing, Stanton?

STANTON (*From the kitchen.*) Cleaning the tiles in your kitchen. They were filthy. (*Returning.*) If I leave you nothing else I'll leave you a clean kitchen and a hoovered flat. And your records! Didn't anyone ever teach you how to look after records? You hold the edges, don't touch the surface with your fingers and always, always, always, put them back in their sleeves. You've unobtainable Morgana Kings lying around being scratched to pieces by Johnny Mathis. Those are artists and you're ruining their life's work, and –

> *ROSIE flares up. Snatches record from him.*

ROSIE You don't like my flat you can clear out. And you leave my kitchen be. I'll clean it when I'm ready, when I don't have to have a flatmate, when I've got the time, when I've got the money and the peace of mind and someone to look at it and – no! (*Returns the record.*) No! Take it back! Clean them! Everything! Touch everything of mine. I love you looking after me. I want your presence in every corner – oh –

> *He takes her in his arms.*

What am I going to do? What, what, what am I going to do?

STANTON (*Taking control.*) It's the dinner party in two days' time, so we have to do the shopping for it tomorrow. Mustn't leave things to the last moment.

> *He pulls her down to the cushions, gently plies her with kisses while he recites:*

Organisation! The secret of cooking is organisation.
Wash up immediately you finish with a utensil. Lay
all your ingredients out before you prepare. Boil
water while you slice onions. Season and soak your
meat while the onions fry. Mix your fillings in the
morning. Prepare your pastry the day before. And
remember, don't go shopping at six for a meal to
which you've invited friends for seven thirty. Now,
where shall we shop?

SCENE 4

*Zabar's deli. But unlit yet. ROSIE is leading STANTON in
with his eyes closed.*

ROSIE   Okay. Now keep your eyes closed. Imagine you're
blind. I'll lead you so you won't fall. You know you
can trust me. I wouldn't let one tiny thing hurt that
person of yours. Every limb, every drop of blood is
precious to me. Okay. Now! Open!

*STANTON opens his eyes as though in wonderland.
Lights full up.*

*Copper utensils hanging, salamis, jars, boxes, a various
array of breads, deli-dishes, cakes – a fantastic shop
alive with shapes, colours, food. A riot of Jewish/
Italian New York.*

STANTON   Rosie! Oh, Rosie!

ROSIE   Like it, huh? Isn't this something? Now here I *have*
to be careful. Here's where I get orgasms which my
therapist says are the more dangerous variety. Look
at that bread. You seen bread like that before? I
mean, don't you just want to go berserk? First there's
the goodies I want to eat here and now. Then there's
the goodies I want to take home with me. Then
there's the goodies I want to buy for friends. And
before I know it I've blown my week's wages. Have
you ever observed the relationship between food
and sex? I mean you take food –

STANTON   Rosie! This is driving me mad. I've got to taste
           something – salami, cheese, a pickle, something!

> *ROSIE is delighted with his delight, and draws him to
> the cheese counter behind which is an ASSISTANT.*

ROSIE   Come. (*To ASSISTANT.*) Okay. Now, my friend from
           England here is made speechless by your shop, and
           speech will not return until a morsel of your most
           exceptional cheese passes his lips. What's your
           suggestion?

> *The grinning female ASSISTANT cuts with a huge
> knife.*

ASSISTANT He from England? I got a cousin lives in England.
           Here. Try this.

> *STANTON takes, tastes.*

> *ASSISTANT gives a second piece to ROSIE.*

A little-known cheese from southern Italy.

ROSIE   (*Savouring.*) Oh, my God. That's bliss. Now *that* – is
           bliss. Stanton?

STANTON   I'm overwhelmed. Let's go. You attack the breads
           and cakes, the salamis and cheese. I'll go for the cuts
           of meat, the deli stuff and the fruit. Agreed?

> *STANTON rushes off.*

> *ROSIE can see the ASSISTANT is impressed.*

ROSIE   Special, huh?

ASSISTANT Special is not the word. He's not afraid of women. In
           New York that's more than special – it's unnatural.
           Where d'you find yourself such a present?

ROSIE   He likes American literature. What can I tell you!

ASSISTANT You bewilder me. Explain.

ROSIE   Take too long.

> *STANTON reappears with a bottle of champagne and
> three glasses.*

Jesus, Stanton, it's the middle of the day. This is decadence.

He pours for them.

ASSISTANT You crazy? You want me to lose my job?

STANTON We are given but one life to live. Take risks! Lechayim!

(*They drink.*)

ROSIE I love you, cuckoo. You take my breath away and give me palpitations. And I swear to you *no* one's ever done that. (*Raising glass.*) May you always be unpredictable.

STANTON And may you always be as loved.

ASSISTANT And may I always have such dangerous customers.

They drink.

STANTON wanders off, swigging from the bottle.

Funny people, the English. Noble but poor. Poor, you know what I mean? Not many cars and no baths in the houses. But they speak the language. You gotta give them that, they speak the language like they invented it.

SCENE 5

The Porno-movie House. Two seats facing us, ROSIE and STANTON with popcorn.

They're laughing and embarrassed like naughty kids. They're waiting for the show to begin.

ROSIE (*Glancing round.*) I think they've opened it just for us, honey.

STANTON This is going to be very tatty and corny, you do realise?

ROSIE Not for me. Not the first time. All first times are an experience.

STANTON   If only the movie houses weren't so seedy I wouldn't feel so guilty.

ROSIE   Watcha feeling guilty about? You're with your mummy. (*Pause.*) How's ma fella?

STANTON   (*Looking round.*) Which one?

ROSIE   Creep! There's only one fella in my life.

She glances down.

STANTON   Rosie, can we make a deal? No touching in this film.

ROSIE   Not even holding hands?

STANTON   Not even –

Lights go down.

ROSIE throws popcorn into her mouth with greater speed.

ROSIE   Sssh! Here we go.

STANTON   Look at that! Even in porno-movies the makers are Jewish.

ROSIE   And we'll soon see if the actors are!

The film begins.

To accompany the flickering is the heaving and puffing of cheap passion, exaggerated, like the smell of cheap scent.

ROSIE and STANTON freeze. They can't believe what they're seeing.

Incredulity, gasps, bewilderment.

Some scenes are so dark they even lean forward trying to understand what's taking place. Hilarious.

Then:

SCENE 6

Disco music!

The disco. Dark. Mirrored walls. Cushioned areas. Constantly moving lights.

The music is loud but the best of its kind. Impossible not to feel young to it.

STANTON and ROSIE are on the floor, both high with pleasure. She moves beautifully of course. And he, surprisingly, moves imaginatively and energetically – which is his failing: he's too energetic. Not absurd but exaggerated.

As a number is changing she stops.

ROSIE (*Commanding.*) Here!

STANTON Of course here.

　　　　　　They embrace and sway, till –

ROSIE Okay. Now, honey. You're a great mover, I mean it. You're Jewish and English, everything against you but you're doing fine, just fine. Only a few tips. There's more than one beat in disco. You hear this one? It's fast, yes? You dance to that and they'll carry you out. But you hear the slow beat? (*Moves to it.*) It's subtler. Easy, easy. And move more from the hips. Keep the top straight. You're flying around too much. On a full floor you could knock someone unconscious.

　　　　　　He succeeds in following her subtler movements. They move as one. He's thrilled, takes balletic risks, twists and swirls. She's bursting with pleasure at his pleasure. The music changes to a more dynamic beat and they really go, take off. Neither can sustain the pace though. They collapse onto the huge cushions, exhausted, panting.

STANTON My heart. Feel it. (*Takes her hand to it.*) Not worked like that in years.

ROSIE Oh, honey, that's unbelievable. No heart should pump like that.

STANTON   Rosie, Rosie, Rosie! How can I go back to normal living after this?

ROSIE   Then stay with me, Stanton, stay. I'd do such things for you. Such marvellous wonderful things.

STANTON   Do you know what it's like moving your body the right way for the first time? I soared, Rosie, soared!

ROSIE   Stay, Stanton, stay!

STANTON   Why haven't I danced more? Everyone should dance. Taught at school, compulsory, with imagination, grace, dynamic – oh, Rosie. My heart!

ROSIE   Stay with me, Stanton.

STANTON   It won't stop. It races on.

ROSIE   It's not the dancing, Stanton, it's love.

STANTON   I think I'm going to have a heart attack.

> *He crashes back.*
>
> *ROSIE drops to him, kissing him, kissing.*

ROSIE   You'll never find anyone to adore you like I do. Stay, Stanton, stay.

STANTON   I'm in a weak state, Rosie. Don't be cruel.

ROSIE   Every part of me is alive. Stay! Stay!

STANTON   I'm tired of myself, Rosie, so tired of my thoughts, my habits, what's expected of me.

ROSIE   Stay! Stay!

STANTON   Every time I catch up with myself I'm not there anyway.

ROSIE   Stay, honey, stay!

STANTON   I have this overwhelming desire to be different. Change my skin, disappear from everyone I know, everything I am, everything I feel.

ROSIE   Stay! Marry me, and stay!

STANTON   Tonight I want to say 'yes'. But on the plane I kept remembering – when I'm sixty she'll be forty-six.

ROSIE   (*Frantic.*) What do I care, what do I *care*! I want you,
          your children *and* your old age.

STANTON   Let's dance.

ROSIE   (*Rolling away.*) Oh, what will I do, what will I *do*?

SCENE 7

Outside Sardi's Restaurant.

*Next day. They've been shopping. They're tired. They've set
down bags. Subdued, too.*

STANTON   Here?

ROSIE   (*Unenthusiastically.*) Yeah! Why not! Fill the entire
          fuckin' city with places I won't be able to visit again.

          *He tries in this embrace to console her. She's inconsolable
          and breaks away, frustrated rather than angry.*

          A WOMAN is about to enter Sardi's.

STANTON   (*Stopping her.*) Excuse me, Miss Minnelli, can I have
          your autograph, please?

ROSIE   Jesus Christ! I've brought a nut into the country.

WOMAN   Minnelli??!!!

ROSIE   (*To WOMAN.*) He's not mine, lady.

          The WOMAN enters.

STANTON   And I say it's a play about Iago's villainy and
          Othello's poor powers of judgement.

ROSIE   How so?

STANTON   Within seconds of Iago pouring the poison of doubt
          into his ear Othello misjudges both Desdemona *and*
          Iago by believing him and not believing her. Within
          seconds.

ROSIE   Not seconds. Iago worked hard.

STANTON   Took him a mere page and a half.

ROSIE   Into which Shakespeare packs more incredible
        dynamite it would take a lesser playwright ten pages
        to pack.

STANTON   What an interestingly structured sentence.

ROSIE   Shithead!

> *He embraces her again. She remains inconsolable.*

What the hell did we think we were doing anyway!
Nothing was right, was it? You're English, I'm
American; you're a Londoner, I'm a New Yorker;
you're a professor, I'm a student; I'm Catholic,
you're Jewish…

STANTON   …I'm male, you're female…

ROSIE   And to cap it all, as if we wouldn't have had enough
        to cause fights, you're black and I'm white… I
        mean… I'm… Oh, fuck it!

STANTON   She's colour-blind.

ROSIE   Don't make jokes! I'm serious.

STANTON   All this time she's imagined she's white…

ROSIE   I'll beat your fuckin' brains out!

STANTON   You're making a scene in public again.

ROSIE   Sorry.

STANTON   But I don't mind. You give vulgarity a human face.

ROSIE   Stop mocking me! I'll tear you limb from fuckin'
        limb.

> *He kisses her again to show he's not mocking her.*
>
> *She buries her head in his neck.*

Stay, Stanton, stay with me.

SCENE 8

FRANCESCA's restaurant. That evening.

STANTON and ROSIE holding hands, dejected, resigned, waiting to be served.

FRANCESCA arrives.

FRANCESCA You ready to order yet?

No response.

Okay. Take you time. You're my only customers and you know what? It feels like you're my only customers for the night. Want some music?

No response.

Okay. I'll play you some music. What would you like? Music to go *with* the mood or against the mood.

No response.

Okay. *With* the mood. You want the classics? The pops? The classic classics? The pop classics? The pop pops? The classical pops?

No response.

Okay. I'll aim it high – the classical classics. You want early? You want Renaissance? You want Romantic? You want modern?

No response.

Okay. I'll go for broke – something so early you won't know what hit you.

She disappears. Silence. Then – Guillaume de Machaut's Messe de Notre Dame.

After some moments –

Blackout!

Screams!

FRANCESCA (VO) No panic! No panic! It's only a power failure.

ROSIE Is it here or everywhere?

STANTON No street lights. Must be everywhere.

FRANCESCA appears with candles.

FRANCESCA It's like 1965 all over again. Remember 1965? Biggest power failure ever.

Sounds of street voices and smashing glass.

Stay calm! Everything's under control. Don't panic.

ROSIE (*Rising, grabbing coats.*) Francesca, I'm gonna panic. And if you take my tip you'll panic too and lock up.

STANTON Where we going? We're safe here.

ROSIE Don't argue with me. I *do* remember 1965. Looting! Fires! Bodily assault. Come! I know my city. Sorry, Francesca.

Sound of police cars. Sound of fire engines.

Headlights and blue lights flash across the stage.

SCENE 9

Street of New York.

Sounds of running, shouting, screaming. It is a riot.

MAN (VO) (*Off.*) Beat it! Get the hell away from this store. Anyone touch this store they get this across their back. You hear me out there? You fuckin' hear?

1ST BOY (VO) Okay, man, no sweat. We don't want no trouble, just loot, man, just easy loot.

2ND BOY (VO) Hey, man, can't see, man. Gotta see, man.

Whoosh of ignited paraffin. Flames.

Can see now, man. See plenty. In we go.

ROSIE'S VOICE Okay, brothers, where's the action?

1ST BOY (VO) All around you, sister, all around, the Lord be praised.

ROSIE (VO) Hal-lelujah! Hal-lelujah!

ROSIE appears, pulling STANTON into doorway. They're breathless from running.

ROSIE   Know the right jargon, you survive.

STANTON   You don't sound sympathetic.

ROSIE   Sympathetic? For *what*? We'll be lucky to come out of this alive. Another gang comes *I* don't know *you*, *you* don't know *me*. Okay? Strangers!

STANTON   'The cock shall not crow till thou hast denied me thrice.'

ROSIE   Don't be gospel-smart with me, mister. I know this area, I know these mentalities, I know these moods.

STANTON   Would you really deny me?

ROSIE   (*Tender.*) Oh no, honey, no! That was just my black humour. Mamma will protect you.

          She stands protectively in front of him, surveying up and down the street.

          Sounds of frantic skirmishing as in war.

          His hands creep from behind her to cup each breast.

          You have exactly three hours to remove your hands.

          He turns her around. They kiss. Sound of a huge crash. He wants to run. She holds him back.

          Safer here.

          Pause as they listen.

ROSIE   They've gone berserk.

STANTON   High unemployment, slum conditions, neglect, indifference – it's understandable.

ROSIE   Understandable, huh?

STANTON   Turn out the lights and look what happens.

ROSIE   Oh? And what *do* you see happening?

STANTON   In a word?

ROSIE   Or two.

STANTON   In a word or two I see around me looting and arson as an expression of rage.

ROSIE   Do you, now?

STANTON   As an expression of rage from a minority youth who feel hopeless members of a helpless community.

ROSIE   Rage? Seemed to me they were having the time of their lives, mister.

STANTON   (*Surprised with this unfashionable view.*) You don't see them as victims of apathy? You don't see all this as revenge, desperation, pent-up torment?

ROSIE   Pent-up torment? Cant! They're positively intoxicated with their dumb, fuckin' luck. Desperation? Cant! I don't see all this taking place in slums. Revenge? Cant! Revenge on who? Spicks and niggers with small shops? The poor, fuckin' long-suffering New Yorker whose city taxes have been spent plenty on social schemes? Don't tell me – I was once a social worker! Look!

They look offstage. ROSIE calls out.

Hey there, fellas. I'm a reporter from the *Star*. Why you stealin' from your own kind, man?

1ST YOUTH (VO)   I ain't stealin', sister. This is lootin'. Root toot de toot lootin'.

ROSIE   That's stealin' in my book, sonny.

2ND YOUTH (VO)   It's the name of the game, lady.

1ST YOUTH (VO)   Aw, Jesus, man, let's go now, we gotta go.

Sound of feet running off.

ROSIE   (*Ferocious mockery.*) 'And we got permission, man, we got permission from all you white liberals cos you told us being black and poor is good enough reason for being lawless. Yes, sir, thank you, sir, we're specially greedy and specially insensitive and specially immoral on account of underprivilege, thank you. We's anti-social cos we don't know no better, thank you. We loot and burn cos we's inferior, yes, sir, thank you, sir! That's just the go-ahead we need. Thank you, thank you.'

She's almost in tears. Controls herself to continue.

But *you* lived in slums, *you* were poor – Jewish East End ghetto and all that – did you loot? Did you burn? Right! Nor did I. So what makes you think you're better? How come *you* had standards but you think *they* can't have standards? How come your mother gave you self-respect but you don't think their mothers could give them self-respect? What makes you think being black exempts them from honesty? You know what you're saying? They're not fully enough human to be held morally responsible for their own behaviour, that's what you're saying. And you know what that makes you? That makes you a racist! A fuckin', patronising, liberal racist.

STANTON has been regarding her with growing, loving admiration.

STANTON   Do you think we can make love here, now, in this doorway?

ROSIE   It'll be our last fuck, ever. Now – run!

She grabs his hand and they run.

SCENE 10

ROSIE's apartment.

The dinner party. Table laid. Candles waiting to be lit. Soft music.

STANTON appears in a suit, struggling with his tie. When it's tied he uncorks a bottle. Pours two glasses.

ROSIE appears in a beautiful black dress. She's stunning but – dreamy in a resigned way.

STANTON   Rosie, you're breathtaking.

He gives her a glass.

ROSIE   Stay, Stanton, stay.

STANTON   Think we bought enough food?

ROSIE   Stay! I'll feed you honey, massage your neck every night…

STANTON   Will I like your friends?

ROSIE   …I'll be your researcher, I'll write your lectures…

STANTON   Think we can take the covers off the plates now?

ROSIE   …I won't scream in public and I'll be beautiful for you every day. Stay with me, Stanton.

STANTON   Dance?

They move around the lounge kissing between times, passionately, unhappily, desperately, hopelessly. A slow ballet around the room.

Over it, for the last time, JUDITH'S VOICE, sad and gentle.

JUDITH (VO)   Oh, you'll have such a lovely time. Eventful and sweetly sad. You can make every hour an event when it's only over twelve days. Rather more difficult, I find, over twenty years. How lucky she'll be. You ought not to stay longer than twelve days with her, Stanton. That way she'll have the illusion it would *all* have been like that. Are you listening? Wake up. It's the midnight reflective hour, dear listeners, and this is your radio midnight friend, Judy Myers, delivering it to you. Did you look forward in middle age to those holidays with your husband, exploring new lands and sights together? Did you look forward to a new release, a fresh start, becoming lovers again. Ah, dear listeners, ah…

ROSIE   Stay, Stanton, stay!

STANTON   The dying words of a famous British actress: 'We didn't rehearse it like this.'

ROSIE   She's had a fair share of you.

STANTON   The dying words of Lytton Strachey: 'Well, if this is dying I don't think much of it.'

ROSIE   Do you know how difficult it is to find a man worth living even a bit of a life with? This entire fuckin' city is full of women without men.

STANTON   Overheard in a Chinese restaurant: 'It's not the egg-roll, Henry, it's the last five years.'

ROSIE   Oh Christ, what am I gonna do?

STANTON   You'll do, Rosie, what we all do: that which belongs to our nature.

STELLA-BELLA bursts in from her room. She's dressed for the party – idiosyncratically!

STELLA-BELLA   If he's short and with glasses and wearing the wrong coloured shirt, he's mine. You hear me, Rosie? But for Christ's sake don't let him in here. Just give him a large neat whisky. I want him drunk before I see him.

She retreats. STANTON flicks through the records.

STANTON   You know you don't have to come with me to buy my kids' records tomorrow.

ROSIE   It's my last day. I'm not letting you out of my sight.

Music of Jane Olivor.

STANTON   What would you do if I came back in a year's time, or thereabouts?

ROSIE   Drop him, take you! You crazy? There *is* no one else for me. Can't you understand? I don't *want* anyone else crawling over my body.

STANTON   Christ! You make me go weak at the knees, Rosie.

ROSIE   But don't give me false hopes, creep!

STANTON   'Shithead', please.

ROSIE   Shithead! I'd be looking for you every day. There was a boy in college who said to me once, 'I'll call you one Friday for a dinner date.' And, do you know, I watched for him over eight weeks! For eight Fridays I made no dates.

Her mood changes.

But you'd never change your mind. Only big people take risks, burst out of their tight, narrow life…

STANTON That's an incredibly trite observation, to say nothing of inaccurate.

ROSIE (*Mocking.*) To say nothing!

STANTON I kiss close friends, male and female, on the lips – would you tolerate that? I keep open house – would you tolerate that? Some of my friends are failures – could you, in view of how competitive you are, tolerate that?

ROSIE Shithead!

STANTON And as final proof that it's Iago's play and not Othello's, Shakespeare gives Iago more lines.

ROSIE Not true.

STANTON Betcha ten dollars.

ROSIE You're on, shithead.

STANTON Othello has eight hundred and twenty-five lines, Iago has one thousand and seventy-seven and thirteen lines of song.

ROSIE You made that up.

STANTON Disprove me.

> *She reaches for a volume of the Bard's work.*
>
> *Music of Jane Olivor up, lights down to denote the passing of minutes.*
>
> *When lights return STANTON holds out his hand.*

Ten dollars.

ROSIE It still doesn't prove it's Iago's play.

STANTON Ten dollars or a quickie.

ROSIE Oh, you're so smug.

STANTON (*Tenderly.*) I don't *care* about Othello, Rosie. Christ! What does it matter who's right or wrong. Why do you have to compete over everything?

> *The phone rings.*
>
> *ROSIE rises to answer it. She paces backwards and forwards.*

ROSIE   Oh hi, Merle. Yeah! Sure I'm okay. You know me.
Just nursing a broken heart. Yeah. I did! He's leaving
me. The romance is over. Not only is he leaving
me but on the last night he packed. Couldn't wait.
His plane leaves at two thirty and he'd packed six
thirty the evening before. No, no, I'll explain next
week. It's too complicated now. No, of course I'm
not gonna shoot myself. For an Englishman? A
coloniser? You crazy?

Long listening pause.

Oh, Merle. I'm so sorry. Yeah – see ya!

Phone down.

His father's in hospital, dying, wouldn't you know.

Long pause.

You make sure now you tell everyone it was you
rejected me. I don't want any misunderstandings.

She suddenly rushes out of the front door.

STANTON   Rosie! They'll be here any moment. Rosie!

But she's gone.

STELLA-BELLA comes through.

STELLA-BELLA   That was Rosie going, wasn't it?

STANTON nods.

A mess, huh?

STANTON opens his arms in despair.

You sure you doing the right thing?

STANTON is silent.

I know, I know! Who knows what's right till after it's
done? Why do I ask!

STANTON   She *will* come back, won't she?

STELLA-BELLA   How far you think she'll go in that dress?

STANTON   Like that dress, Stella-Bella?

STELLA-BELLA   Crazy about it. You wanna marry me instead?

STANTON   I bought it for her in the middle of the riots. This shop, run by a couple of terrified gays, and there, in the window, this remarkable dress. Very odd feeling dealing with a shopkeeper who takes your money with one hand and wields a hatchet with the other.

STELLA-BELLA   You know you've broken her heart, don't you? She's never, never, never ever been in such a state.

STANTON   Don't make me feel worse than I do.

STELLA-BELLA   I'm confused. Tell me. Why come back at all?

STANTON   To stand at the edge. See if I could jump.

STELLA-BELLA   And you couldn't?

STANTON   I could but –

STELLA-BELLA   But what? You couldn't for Rosie? You weren't overwhelmed by Rosie?

STANTON   Oh, I was, that. Overwhelmed and whelmed over and tossed around and about and up and down and brought to the edge...

She waits for more.

STELLA-BELLA   ...but no jump.

STANTON   No jump.

STELLA-BELLA   Can you say why? The truth now.

Long pause.

STANTON   Sometimes truth is a kind of betrayal.

The doorbell rings.

The guests.

STELLA-BELLA   No. It's her.

STANTON   How do you know it's her?

STELLA-BELLA   It's her! Believe me. (*Returning to her room.*) You can suppress the truth for ever now.

STANTON opens the door. It is ROSIE. She's determinedly revived.

ROSIE   Hello, cuckoo. Miss me? Thought I'd run out on yer, huh? Where's the champagne? You *are* gonna say goodbye to me on champagne, you know. On your last night you're doing what *I* want.

> *She goes to the fridge. Returns with bottle for him to open.*

STANTON   (*Incredulously.*) I was missing you.

ROSIE   (*Tenderly.*) Hurt to be apart, didn't it? Well, you'd better get used to it.

STANTON   Right now I would love a cigarette.

ROSIE   When did you give up?

STANTON   When I started to puff making love.

ROSIE   *I* used to drink a lot. Stopped when I began telling friends the truth.

STANTON   I dreamt about a friend last night. Now what were the details? Can't remember. But as I was coming out of the dream he was saying something to me about 'as sad as a field of mint'. And when I was awake I had this line going round and round in my head: 'They came down off the mountain into a field of melancholy mint.' (*Pause.*) *Is* mint melancholy?

ROSIE   (*Stroking his face.*) We are going to make love all night. Non-stop.

STANTON   What, no breaks at all?

ROSIE   Only to feed you a steak now and then.

STANTON   And what will *you* eat to regain strength?

ROSIE   I'm fourteen years younger, remember?

STANTON   Creep!

ROSIE   Know what I love about you? You're not competitive. The boy I had before you he was competitive. Even in bed. No peace. I've always gone after 'boys', men who were my inferior, so's I could mother them. Well, not anymore. I've touched the heights. From here on I'm not putting up with anyone I don't really care about.

> *Sound of doorbell. Sound of guests. Music changes to Sinatra.*

SCENE 11

ROSIE's apartment.

After the party. After tempestuous love-making.

In the subdued light of a solitary candle ROSIE and STANTON naked on the cushions. Exhausted.

ROSIE pinches herself.

ROSIE   Fleshy, huh?

STANTON   Who thought I'd ever make love to pop music?

ROSIE   Stay, Stanton, stay!

STANTON   I'm dry. My back's broken, I've lost seven pounds, my heart's racing and I'm dry.

> *ROSIE staggers to the kitchen. Fridge door opens, clink of glass, pouring of liquid, bottle returned, fridge door slammed.*
>
> *ROSIE returns with one glass full.*

ROSIE   Soda suit you?

STANTON   Nothing better.

> *She kneels to him, glass to his lips – nurse to a soldier wounded in battle.*
>
> *Suddenly her eyes catch something. STANTON follows what she gazes at. It's his 'fella'. A used, limp, 'fella' is a comic and pathetic sight, worn-out and zonked-looking.*
>
> *ROSIE picks it up by its loose skin between two fingers.*

ROSIE   *What –* is this?

STANTON   Don't know. Wasn't there this morning.

ROSIE   Poor thing. Someone beat you up, little fella?

STANTON   Less of the 'little'.

ROSIE   Don't be offended. Size isn't everything.

        Whistles, as to a dog.

        Up, Rover, up! Good boy! Ah – Rover too tired to
        jump for his bone? Rover been hunting all day?

        *She again picks it up. Lets it drop. Again and
        again.*

STANTON Rosie, it is *not* a piece of meat on a butcher's slab!
        Will you please show a little more respect for the
        service he's done you.

        *ROSIE moves to a surface cluttered with something
        from every room; rummages, extracts from the clutter a
        kid's tin flute, squats cross-legged beside the 'fella' and
        plays, trying to charm the 'snake' to raise its head.*

        *Which sends them both into fits of laughter – from
        which she breaks off and slowly, achingly folds into
        his arms with a moan.*

ROSIE   I can't bear it. I can't bear to think of a *day* without
        you let alone the rest of my life. I want you, your
        children, your gentleness, your patience, your
        forgiveness, your old age, your mind, your laughter,
        your… I'm so angry, Stanton. I *know* you love me,
        I see it from the way you look at me. And you're
        denying it. It's just crazy. Wrong and crazy and no
        one will forgive you.

        He caresses her, soothingly.

STANTON Shush, shush, easy, Rosie, easy.

        *The dawn creeps through closed curtains. They begin
        to dress. ROSIE slips swiftly into a tracksuit.*

ROSIE   You know when it'll really hit me? In about two
        weeks from now. (*Pause.*) Stay and fuckin' marry me,
        Stanton! (*Pause.*) Like talking to a dead horse. What
        the hell was I doing making love with a dead horse.

STANTON (*Taking her in his arms.*) Come here, four eyes.

ROSIE   Who are you calling 'four eyes'?

She snuggles up. Their mood is flat though their humour rolls on.

You'll be all right. A little strain at first, but one by one they'll come round. Judy will forgive you. Your friends will look at you with different eyes, a bit of a hero, the one who almost got away. The children will love you as always. Nothing much will change.

STANTON   I know exactly what it'll be like when I get back. I'll grieve. *You'll* be all right but I – will grieve. You'll meet your friends, make your sunny jokes, pursue your degree studies, hide it all inside. Not me. I'm transparent. That's how the family knew. I came back from the seminar last time and all I did was keep playing your music. Jesus! How could they *not* know. Grieve. Sit shivah. Know what 'shivah' is? After a death the Jews insist on a week in which you do nothing. Everyone who isn't family does it for you. I'll sit shivah. Grieve.

SCENE 12

Airport. Departure gate.

ROSIE in her grey, baggy tracksuit trousers, a yellow sweatshirt, sneakers and her grey 1930s astrakhan coat. She's zany and kid-like.

ROSIE   Hey! Look at the way I walk in sweats.

STANTON   If anyone had ever told me I'd be walking out with a teeny-bopper…

ROSIE   If anyone had told me I'd be seen walking out in sweats! Look, as soon as I wear them I walk a certain way. Can't help myself. Look.

She pushes STANTON ahead so that he can see her; then she walks towards him swaggering like a male athlete into his arms. She clings.

We did a lot in twelve days.

STANTON   Lived a whole life time.

ROSIE   Except we didn't play chess in Washington Square.

STANTON   Damn!

ROSIE   (*Inspecting his face.*) How did all those little blood
            vessels burst on your nose?

STANTON   The effort of it, Rosie, the effort.

ROSIE   I can't *believe* we won't be seeing one another again.
            (*Angry growl.*) Promise me something?

STANTON   Anything.

ROSIE   Promise me you won't be too proud to come back if
            you change your mind.

STANTON   Promise.

ROSIE   Cross your heart.

STANTON   Who, me?

ROSIE   Well, he *was* Jewish, dammit.

            It's time to part.

            *ROSIE and STANTON face each other. They kiss.
            Simply.*

            You take care, now.

STANTON   Study hard, Rosie, promise me?

            Another simple kiss.

ROSIE   Shit! We should have made love in the taxi!

            *He gives her a last simple kiss, turns, and moves
            towards the door.*

            In that instant his back is turned she flees.

            *He turns for a last wave. She has gone. He is
            desolate.*

            Slow, slow, fade of the light.

            END